Hans Rookmaaker:
A Biography

Linette Martin

InterVarsity Press
Downers Grove
Illinois 60515

InterVarsity Press is the book-publishing
division of Inter-Varsity Christian Fellowship,
a student movement active on campus
at hundreds of universities, colleges and
schools of nursing. For information about local
and regional activities, write
IVCF, 233 Langdon St., Madison, WI 53703.

ISBN 0-87784-725-8
Library of Congress Catalog Card Number: 79-2382

Printed in the United States of America

to the Reverend Fred Secombe
Thank you for what I have learned and
unlearned through your ministry

Figure in a Landscape

GRUNTING AND SWEATING, the four young men heaved the chunk of stone out of the van and lowered it to the driveway outside the new chapel. They went back to their work in the community while Wim Rietkerk, the pastor, went to fetch Hans Rookmaaker.

"Professor Rookmaaker, that old font given by the village church has just come. It is said to be eleventh-century."

"So. I come now and take a look."

He sauntered out to the drive, filling his pipe, and stood looking down at the great bowl of grey rock. "Well, it is not eleventh-century, that is certain. Now I wonder, maybe fourteenth? That would be the earliest . . ."

He clicked his fingers absent-mindedly at Wim, "Just turn it round for me so I can see the other side."

Wim exploded. "You say 'Turn it round'? That great thing? I say to you that you should better walk round to the other side yourself!"

Rookmaaker came back to reality, his face falling like that of a little child who had been reprimanded, "Oh, Wim, of course. Forgive me, please; I didn't think." Then his eyes began to twinkle, "Look, I have learned from my mistake already. I am walking round it myself. Yes, I would say maybe it is the fifteenth century. One thing is very sure: it is not as old as the eleventh, no matter who tells you. They are wrong and I am right."

When it came to making up his own mind and sticking to it, Hans Rookmaaker had had plenty of practice. It had not been easy to begin living a Christian life in a Nazi POW camp. It had not been easy to mingle with Protestant Evangelicals in the 1960s and speak of artistic values. (His

9

popularity was once adversely affected when he showed slides of Rubens nudes at a church conference in America.) The man had a stubborn streak and for the influence he was to have on the Evangelical world he was to need all the stubbornness and charm that his countrymen are known for.

According to the myth of national character (if it is a myth) Hans Rookmaaker was typically Dutch. A loyal family man and reserved as an oyster, combining the wit of Thyl Ulenspiegel with the sobriety of the proverbial judge; he inspired equal measures of love and rage. He took time making up his mind, turning every facet of a question to the light, like an Amsterdam diamond merchant examining his wares. When he had made his decision, there was as good a chance of shifting his opinion as there was of flattening the Alps or flooding the Sahara.

When it comes to doing geographical impossibilities, the Dutch have the monopoly over the rest of the world. If other nations want more *lebensraum*, they get it by colonisation or war. The Dutch merely move back the sea. Today, a quarter of the Netherlands lies below sea-level and another quarter is only three feet above it but they still haven't finished draining what they want.

"God made the sea," they tell you, "but the Dutch made the land." It could only have been accomplished by something that Rookmaaker's compatriots are renowned for: a streak of stubbornness that would make a mule look fickle.

If there is such a thing as national character, the biography of one man must begin with the biography of his nation; with the bones of rivers and rocks, the sinews of history. The title of the portrait is not *Individual Man* but *Figure in a Landscape*.

A tulip bulb stays in the ground for a long time before the flower is seen and the Netherlands existed for a long time before its brief Golden Age in the seventeenth century. For its first millennia, the culture was undreamt of that would flower with Thomas à Kempis, Erasmus, Spinoza, Grotius, Vermeer and Leeuwenhoek. The early history of Hans

Rookmaaker's native land is wave-washed and smells of herrings.

By rights Holland should not be a nation at all. It is a flat land, a hollow land, as the name of two of its western provinces suggest. It is where the Rijn and the Maas drain slowly and floodingly off the north-west corner of the Great Plain of Europe into the chilly waters of the North Sea. This is delta country, once touched by an ice-sheet that rolled boulders the size of dinosaurs down from Scandinavia; a place of dunes, wooded islands, bright sun, changing light and watery skies. The climate has been described as like an everlasting April, or a confounded nuisance.

"If you don't like our weather," say the Dutch, "wait a few minutes." They claim their worst weather comes from England. If so, it is probably because the English are glad to get rid of it. Where no hill rises higher than 1000 feet the weather is a fickle lady. Mist and cloud shadow, sun and rain sweep easily over the broad pastures, as the surface of canals shimmers like crêpe under a passing breeze. The view is clear for miles where tiny cumulus clouds meet the rim of the land. The Dutch landscape is all sky, pressing down upon the fields. Every square yard of their land is lived on, cultivated or grazed. It is said of Hans Rookmaaker's country, *"Holland, ge biedt geen ruimt als aan den geest"* (Holland, you offer room for nothing but the spirit).

People have been living in the Low Countries for a very long time. Ancient stone tombs, *hunnebedden,* crouch in the landscape of Drenthe in the north-east, where faience beads from the Egypt of 1400 BC have been dug out of the peat bog. Blond Germanic tribes arrived here after a slow trek from the east. When they got to the lowlands, they dug their heels into the delta mud and put up a stubborn resistance against tough tribes of Celts from the south who tried to push them off the edge. "This far but no further." The land might squelch at every step but the land was theirs. Against long odds (some would say against all reason) they settled in and built small islands of branches and earth for their cows and their wives to retreat to when the tides rolled over the meadows.

11

When Roman soldiers came jingling up from Gaul in the BC fifties to announce that the land was theirs, they found the Lowlanders in the mood for a protracted argument. The argument against raiders was to last, on and off, for four hundred years, when the matter was settled by a combination of marauding seas and waves of tribesmen.

The Romans called the land north of the Rijn "Batavia". They made use of Lowlander mercenaries, hides from Friesian cows were made into Roman sandals that tramped all over the Empire, and the Appian Way was extended through Maastricht. But the land was never really theirs; it was too hostile and too wet. When their Empire crumbled away at the edges, Germanic deities and Germanic ways still ruled the hollow delta. The Latins had tamed the marsh people's tongue as little as they had tamed their lives. Today, Netherlands speech is still linked with those of Britain, Germany and Scandinavia and has the characteristic double "a" as in Rookmaaker.

After the Danish Viking raids and the Saxon invasions the country was still best suited for C. S. Lewis' marsh-dwelling character, Puddleglum. The inhabitants manoeuvred their dug-out canoes between the islands and dunes on the western coast and passed an uncomplicated life with fish and fowl, too stubborn to move over. No-one could have foreseen that the Low Countries would be anything more than a backwater of the European continent.

It was a river and a religion that made the difference. Whoever controlled the mouth of the Rijn, controlled the tradesmen's entrance of Europe. But it was not much use unless you knew how to drain the oozing landscape where the river ran, and there was not much motive for improving things if life was nasty, brutish and without hope.

In the seventh and eighth centuries, saintly men like Lambert, Wilfred, Willibrord, Willehad, Hubert and Boniface preached Christ to the Puddleglums. Then Irish Benedictines settled in, girded up their black robes out of the mud and taught the Dutch efficient methods of poldering and draining the land. The Gospel made a difference in a practical area of life. To this day the Dutch speak of *monnikenwerk* (monk-work) when they want a word for heavy labour.

Norman raids during most of the ninth century destroyed churches and monasteries but the inhabitants of the Low Countries had passed the point of no return. They had moved from tribe to society. They had found a way to turn an honest medieval penny with agriculture and trade. As decades passed into centuries, national identity grew. Tribes learned to sink their differences as they cooperated in building *dijks* against their common enemy, the sea. The masters of the river demanded a toll from every boat that wanted to cross their watery doorstep. Their river-mouth towns grew tougher. In time they took on the waning Hanseatic League that had been monopolising the Baltic ports. What Antwerp lost in importance, Amsterdam gained. When shifts of tide and climate made new herring shoals move into the North Sea, the little sea-ports of Zeeland and Noord- and Zuid-Holland fished and bartered them for a better way of life.

The domestic riches we see in the Dutch interior paintings; the furs and pearls, carpets and inlaid furniture, the jewelled armour that Rembrandt loved to paint, were spawned by an economy based on salted fish. An impossible landscape had produced a practical people.

Their adjective is best: *nuchter*. This *nuchterheid* sobriety can infuriate or refresh, depending on your point of view. It is the quality of having one's feet on the ground without having them stuck in the mud. The followers of the *Devotio Moderna* had a practical streak in their pre-Reformation lay piety. The way Hans Rookmaaker approached the Christian life was similarly *nuchter*.

When the Professor of Art History began to teach Reformed Christians to appreciate art, his countrymen had been doing the impossible for centuries. Just as no-one could have foreseen what the hollow land would become, no-one could have guessed what one man would accomplish in a close-packed life of fifty-five years.

What was he like? The publisher gave me one year to find out. I have sat in Hans Rookmaaker's study, typed on his ancient typewriter, leafed through his Bible and cycled through his countryside. I have talked to his nearest relatives, his severest critics and his dearest friends. Each person knew a little part of the man. Slowly his life-story and character began to emerge from the interviews, diaries, and photo albums. It was like watching a sculptor at work, chipping away excess marble to reveal the finished statue. I also had a strange feeling of watching a Creator at work, chipping away at most unlikely material to shape a man of God.

When I first spoke to Mrs. Rookmaaker about writing the book she said, "Oh, Linette, I'm afraid you make my husband too perfect."

I said, "Don't worry; I won't."

CHAPTER ONE

Roots and Relatives

HANS ROOKMAAKER'S SECOND son, Kees, got the family tree from his father's study. We unfolded it on the dining room table and tried to trace the roots of the man as far down in history as they are known.

The family tree goes back to the 1700s, when Hendrik, a baker of Arnhem married Cornelia of Apeldoorn. The eighteenth century was the Periwig Period of Netherlands history. The Golden Age had passed in a brief flash. The proud navy had shrunk to a handful of ships, flat-bottomed and out-of-date beside the flashy tea clippers that raced around the Dutch-discovered Cape Horn. Once the Netherlands had had the best navy in the world, sailing up the Medway in 1664 to revenge the British for turning Nieuw Amsterdam into New York. By the 1700s the Golden Age was barely a glimmer on the horizon; the hard-won independence from Catholic government had lost its direction and identity. The ruling classes copied the French in all things, even speaking their language in preference to their native Hollands and Friesian dialects. The rank and file copied the ruling classes.

In 1740 the wife of a baker bore him a son, as the wife of the baker's father had once born him. Hans Rookmaaker's family stretched back and back, like the sound of hand-hewn clogs receding into the mist, but the written record begins in the 1760s with the names of Hendrik of Arnhem and Cornelia of Apeldoorn.

There are no professors of art history or even teachers listed among their children or grandchildren. We are confronted by solid generations of bakers, standing shoulder to shoulder like buns on a shelf. Hendrik's brother became a silversmith in Dokkum, Friesland, where he worked on teapots, porringers and horsebridles for fashionable Frieslanders. But apart from him, there is no trace of artistry in the family; they are tradesmen and merchants, the bourgeois backbone of a self-confessed bourgeois land.

At the end of the Periwig century the Low Countries had rearranged themselves into the Batavian Republic. By this time Hendrik and Cornelia's grandchildren had acquired the name Klaverwiede and the *klaver* (clover) was featured on the family crest, flanked by two lions rampant and topped by a crown.

A British family would enjoy claiming Royal connections at the baker's shop. I asked Kees about the crown but he waved my enquiry aside. "Oh, that's nothing in the Netherlands; we all have that on our crests."

Van Klaver or Klaverwiede was an unusual name for a baker in the eighteenth century. Surnames were not generally used then in the Netherlands. Most people, I learned, still followed the ancient custom of identifying themselves by the name of their village, like Thomas à Kempis or Rembrandt van Rijn. Though aristocracy has always been concerned with family lines, the mass of the people do not find its identity in blood but in place of occupation.

This state of affairs was not tidy enough for the Napoleonic regime when it absorbed the Batavian Republic. It was proclaimed that every citizen should have a proper surname. The Dutch responded to that piece of Gallic bureaucratic nonsense by inventing names for each other that could barely be said with a straight face; names like High-bosom, Horror or Born-naked.

About this time, so the story goes, van Klaver of Arnhem improved the design of his baker's oven so the fire would draw better. His neighbours called him Rookmaaker—smoke-maker—and the name stuck. For Hans Roelof Rookmaaker, the twentieth-century professor of Amsterdam, the name is delightfully appropriate: he was rarely seen in adult life without his pipe. But as his critics were to discover, it was often a case of *geen rook zonder vuur* (no smoke without fire).

After the Napoleonic days, several of the smoke-making clan moved a hundred kilometres west to Haarlem where the first one to be named Roelof inched a little higher up the social ladder by becoming a wine merchant. From the 1860s, other place names begin to appear on the family tree. Hans' grandfather, one of the self-improved men of the nineteenth century, was an Assistant Resident in the East Indies, helping the Resident to govern as official representative of King William III. (Not the British William III. Theirs. He reigned from 1849 to 1890.)

In the late sixteenth century the Netherlanders had snatched their exotic colony away from Portugal who had claimed the islands for the previous hundred years. The Dutch battled off the English traders by fair means and foul. Bit by bit the East Indies became the Dutch East Indies, adding a spice of life to the Low Countries economy in its Golden Age. Relationships between Dutch, British and native Indonesians remained touchy. Too often the cash crops of hungry islanders lined the pockets of the Europeans. The Dutch introduced rubber trees from the Amazon in the 1870s and supplied the growing motor industry. Diplomats, civil servants and plantation owners developed a predictable sub-culture, living in beautiful houses like the one in which Hans Rookmaaker spent part of his wandering childhood.

"Oh, east is east and west is west," wrote Kipling in 1889, "and never the twain shall meet, till Earth and Sky stand presently at God's great Judgement Seat." The Dutch did for the native Indonesians what the British Raj did for the Indians: no less and no more.

Assistant Resident Rookmaaker, Hans' grandfather, was from a Protestant family but he took to himself a Catholic wife. At his wedding the bridegroom announced that there would be no trouble because there would be no more church-going for either of them. Nine Rookmaaker children were born in the Spice Islands at two-year intervals during the closing years of the nineteenth century. Their birthplaces listed on the family tree tell an unwritten tale of rootless colonial life. The Assistant Resident, working hard for his honourable title, moved his wife and increasing brood from place to place between Java, Sumatra and Celebes. In 1887 the eighth child and fourth son was born. He was the Henderik who was to become the father of the man that Birmingham art students called "Rooky".

In Henderik's childhood, things were going fairly well in the Colonies. If his life had lasted four years longer he would have seen the Dutch Empire brought to an end. Henderik was a colonial born and bred. While still a young man, he rose higher than his father by becoming Resident.

The colonial Rookmaaker's parental home is Den Haag in Zuid-Holland. It is a city of Government offices, of the Queen and of all diplomats, both aspiring and retiring. The city has arched eyebrows and a gracious smile. It will not be flurried. The nearest English equivalent to Den Haag is Cheltenham Spa. The American equivalent does not exist.

Henderik Rookmaaker met Theodora Catherine Heitink in Den Haag. She was from a good family, she was clever and she had red-gold hair. He married her on August 25th 1911 and swept her off to the Lamponsche District in South Sumatra. It was very different from Den Haag. Until only fifty years before, the Lamponsche area had been ill-reputed as a place of slave-trading and piracy.

The bride had to manage as best she could as an inexperienced young wife and hostess of twenty-one years old. She was cut off from contact with other Europeans at four degrees south of the steamy Equator; isolated between jungle and rubber plantation in a white house with a flagpole on the front lawn. The Dutch flag was flown whenever her husband happened to be at home. Theodora was expected to cope with her new life as a woman of means, ruling over a houseful of obsequiousness; the pukka colonial wife.

She barely succeeded. A daughter was born at the end of November 1912, and sixteen months later, to her husband's disappointment, another daughter. Mevr. Rookmaaker's condition was described vaguely as "nerves", though the vomiting and fainting fits were real enough. She had to spend the greater part of each pregnancy lying down, while the twenty-five-year-old Resident sat at one end of his elegantly laid table, staring at her empty chair.

The girls, Henrietta and Theodora, grew to seven and six years old, their schooling conditioned by their status as colonial children. Their mother's attempts to teach them at home ended in failure. School in the Netherlands was the only solution and the family moved back there in 1920, the Resident looking pleasantly on his two girls, but wishing for the traditional son and heir.

Then word spread that Mevr. Rookmaaker was once again "in a delicate condition". Her nerves had travelled back with her from the rubber plantations and, once again, she had to spend the greater part of her pregnancy lying down. Third time lucky. It was a boy. Theodora Catherine's existence on the family tree was justified and the Resident's ambitions and dreams were centred on young Henderik Roelof Rookmaaker who was known as Hans. He was born in Den Haag on Monday, February 27th 1922.

"I do not know if my parents wanted to have more children," said the elder daughter bluntly in adult life, "I think Hans was an accident."

His sister Dora, then nine years old, remembered her first sight of the new baby in the hospital crib. "He was tiny and red all over. He looked like a little old man. I told my mother I did not much like the look of him." Luckily the first impression faded and brother and sister were close friends throughout his life.

Hans crawled at seven months and walked at nine months. By three years he was as active as a little monkey, spoiled outrageously all the way.

"Mother," said Dora, "I believe if that little boy asked you for his very own Mercedes-Benz, you would give it to him."

"Why, yes, I would."

During his childhood, the family shuttled between Den Haag and Sumatra, the sea trip via the Suez Canal taking several weeks each time. His mother's nerves never left her. When they moved into the Resident's Palace with its marble pillared portico and swimming pool (the ultimate luxury in the 1930s) she took to roaming from house to house visiting friends. She would leave at 9.00, return for lunch and go roaming again till the evening meal. She was never there when the girls needed her. They were raised by servants.

As young Hans grew, his first steps were taken with his sisters. Increasingly, he took his joys and troubles to Dora. She recognised her own need of mothering and tried to make up to her brother what she had lacked. When they were once again in Den Haag, it was Dora who walked Hans to school and fetched him home for tea.

Mevr. Rookmaaker-Heitink put on weight, posed for pictures in front of the marble pillars in Sumatra and doted on her children from a safe distance. She was a woman of many questions.

"Who was at the party, Hansje? What did you eat? What games did you play? What did you say—do—think? Tell me, Hansje, tell me!" Hans closed up like a Noordzee mussel.

When she was not hounding them with questions, their mother was always proper, cool and controlled, but who wants a mother like that? The children found their security in their marbled home, with oriental rugs and native carvings and brass. There they acquired a graciousness that never left them. Servants with bland brown faces bowed aside for them in every doorway. Belgian and Dutch nobility came to dinner and young Hans was allowed to sit up late on those occasions with his very own small glass of beer to sip with the grown-ups and their wine.

In time the Resident caused a swimming pavilion to be built in the Palace gardens and tennis courts were laid out behind it. He had the best view landscaped. There were parties nearly every weekend with neighbouring diplomatic families. Part of the grounds were graciously given (or given back) to native Indonesians for their own use.

Hennie, Dora and Hans got on well with their father, accompanying him on hunting trips into the jungle to shoot boar, deer, python and tiger and be photographed by the hot geysers. Tigers were unusual and it was an exciting moment when servants ran in to announce that big cat footprints had been found in the garden.

Once a year on August 31st the Resident dressed in a navy-blue uniform with medals to receive the congratulations of grateful Indonesian subjects on the birthday of Queen Wilhelmina.

As Dora turned the pages of the well-worn family album, I asked about the two medals resplendent against her father's chest in the sepia photograph. One of them, the Leopold Order, was pure diplomacy. Prince Leopold of the Belgians enjoyed being shown over Florus Island by the Resident and he pinned a medal on him by way of a thank you. Since the year was 1930, a century after Belgium broke away from the Netherlands to form her own nation, the medal was the sort of commemorative gesture that princes and diplomats revel in. Later Henderik visited the Royal Family in Brussels where he got on well with Queen Astrid.

"The other was the Oranje-Nassau medal," said Dora, "He got that for arranging the migration of Javanese people to South Sumatra. They were very poor and my father arranged for them to move where there was land open. It didn't cost the Dutch Government a penny because my father did it all by loan and the Indonesians paid it all back when they were settled."

Among photos of the Resident's wife and daughters in spotless tennis clothes is a snap of Indonesians tangled together in the harbour, their entire villages uprooted in search of more promising rice fields. The docile native children in the picture belonged to the generation that rose up in rebellion after the war. Between 1945 and 1949 that generation set upon their masters' palatial homes, reducing them to smoking rubble.

Resident Rookmaaker did not live to see the twilight of the colonial gods. Some Indonesian nationalist groups had arisen during the twenties, one of them led by a young man called Sukharno, but the Resident still felt secure. He posed for his picture in uniform and medals; a close-packed little man with round head, rimless glasses, big mouth and prominent nose; a man used to being obeyed.

21

In June 1936 he was retired early because of ill-health and the family moved to a small flat-fronted Den Haag house with a small back garden. Then he and his wife were sent to Japan while the children were palmed off onto various relatives with varying success. After a year they were reunited in Den Haag.

In 1940 war came to the Rookmaakers' neutral country. The middle-aged ex-Resident, a model of diplomacy, managed to avoid both collaboration and resistance, but he and his wife were not allowed to sit out the Occupation in dignified detachment. The Nazis wanted to drive a tank-road through their home so they had to move again.

The war scattered his family. Dora and her husband were interned by the Japanese in Indonesia. Hans, the favoured son, was imprisoned in Poland. The long, cold winter of 1944–45 in the occupied Netherlands was a different world from Sumatra of the twenties. On January 31st 1945 the fifty-seven-year-old ex-Resident, his medals laid away for safe keeping, had a heart attack from the exertion of chopping wood for his own fire. Neither doctor nor ambulance could be found on that snowy day but it didn't matter; he was dead in five minutes.

When Hans returned home from the war, his mother knew her son was different from the way she had remembered him. He had become religious, a thing that was not encouraged in the proper diplomatic world. There had been a sudden interest in religion when he had been released from a Nazi prison at eighteen, but this time it seemed to have set in permanently. He kept reading the Bible. It was disconcerting. There had been no Bible in the Resident's Palace, and during the intermittent times they had been living in Den Haag, church-going had been a sudden, social event, riddled by a vague sense of guilt.

"Nonsense, Theodora," Henderik would say, struggling with his collar stud, "of course we must take the children to church once in a while. Whatever will people think?"

Theodora had been brought up without religion but she obeyed her husband, and called a servant to get the children into their best clothes. Church once in a while was all there ever was, and in between those whiles the safe, diplomatic world rolled on as smoothly as the ripples in the Palace swimming pool.

When the two girls had been babies, a Dutch missionary had happened to pass through the Lamponsche District and the Resident, conscious of doing the right thing, sent for the man and had the girls baptised. No missionary happened to pass by when there were three children in the Palace so Hans Roelof Rookmaaker did not receive Christian baptism till his adult life.

When he first came home from the war in 1945, he was different. It was something for his friends to talk about among themselves. One of them, Marcus' girl, dropped by to visit Hans' mother and before long the conversation turned to the religiosity of Hans.

"Never mind, Mevr. Rookmaaker," she said, "he is young, even younger than me. He will get over it. He will change back."

But Theodora shook her head in a moment of insight, "No. I know my Hansje. He will never change."

In 1962 his mother's mind fell gently apart. Her daughter-in-law offered to make a home for her but the doctor advised against it. "With young children in the household it would be impossible." So the Resident's wife spent the last ten years of her life in the bare room of a psychiatric nursing home. Her daughters took it in turns with her son to take her for a walk on Sunday afternoons or to sit with her. Conversation was not easy, but then it never had been.

Towards the end Hans visited her nearly every week, though humanly speaking it was a waste of time. Five minutes after he had left the room, she could not remember that he had ever been there. When she died at eighty-two, the officials of the nursing home said they had nowhere to keep her body till the funeral. So for the last three days, before she was laid to rest beside her husband in Den Haag's graveyard, Theodora Catherine Rookmaaker-Heitink of the marble portico had to be moved once again.

CHAPTER TWO

The Son of the Resident

AS I WATCHED, Dora leafed through albums of family photographs. They were small sepia memories of another world: houses that no longer exist, clothes that are no longer worn and people whose names have been forgotten. On one page there was a picture of a little child in a white vest, standing at his mother's knee, both parents and sisters smiling determinedly at the cameraman whose shadow spills out towards them over the grass. It was my first sight of young Hans.

The picture must have been taken soon after they returned to Indonesia, for he spent the first three years of his life in Den Haag, celebrating Sinterklaas Day in that land of clogs and mist. The practical Dutch separate the religious festival of Christmas from the present-giving by celebrating St. Nicolas Day. That leaves December 25th free as a day of worship for those who still have someone to worship. Sinterklaas, patron of sailors, children and pawnbrokers, is fêted on December 6th. Fond and foolish stories have been woven around the fourth-century Bishop of Asia Minor. All that the Reformed children know is that he represents presents and fun. A painting by Jan Steen that hangs in the Amsterdam Rijksmuseum shows a Sinterklaas Day in the 1600s. Each child has a present, even the one who is at first teased with a birch whip in a wooden shoe.

There was no such teasing in the Rookmaaker household; only lavish gifts and love. Midnight struck in the house as Mevr. Rookmaaker hurried upstairs to wake little Hans.

"Come, I promised you I would wake you for Sinterklaas. Oh, my little son, so sleepy. Here, put your arms round my neck; I will carry you down. Awake now? There, see what

Sinterklaas has brought you. Oh, so many pretty things!"

Deposited gently in the middle of the family circle, the brown-eyed child gazed solemnly at the pile of gifts. He blinked, still dazed by the lights and laughter.

Hennie leaned towards him, "See, Hansje, this is for you. Come, sit by me and open it so we can all see what it is."

"Mine?"

"Yes, dear, its yours. Sinterklaas brought it."

"Open it, Hansje, let's see!"

He glanced at his parents and sisters, wrapped his skinny arms round his present and padded upstairs to his room. Laughing, they called him back. After a long interval he returned.

"What have you done with your present? We wanted to see!"

"In my bed."

"Well, this is a big present. You will let us see you open this—"

No, he wouldn't. He grabbed it and waddled off again, his large flat feet turned out like a duck; a determined little figure in a white nightgown puffing up the steep Dutch stairs with his arms full. He opened his presents alone and enjoyed the first sight of them alone before he shared them with his family.

Typical? Later it was remembered as being typical. A subsequent childhood in which he was brought up by a succession of servants, built upon that foundation of natural shyness. He grew up to be a man who longed for close relationships but who found them hard to initiate or cope with. The small child in the white nightshirt became an adult who was at home in a scholar's world, in which every object is inanimate as a framed painting, and every fact can be filed away in a predictable place.

Before long the Sinterklaas presents and all the other current belongings of his childhood were packed into steamer trunks labelled Sumatra. They left Beeklaan 311 with the dunes nearby, the dark stairways between the houses that Dora ran past on dark evenings, and the glorious-smelling Rademaaker chocolate factory at the end of the road. The girls had been out to Indonesia twice before. It was the first time for the Son of the Resident.

There he was fêted at once by the servants of a house in Fort de Kock, built for European colonials on the west coast of Sumatra. He explored the big, light rooms, trotting after Dora over polished wood floors and oriental carpets. He stared wide-eyed at the smooth brown-faced people who lifted him into his high chair and offered him rice cooked in oil and milk. He found in his childish way that grass growing in the East Indies was the same as grass growing in Zuid-Holland. He learned there were always people nearby to pick him up when he fell down.

"Mummy?"

"No, Hansje, Mummy's gone out to see friends." His twelve-year-old sister hoisted the little boy onto her hip and walked him towards the dappled light under the palm trees. "You must learn to play in the shade when we live here."

"Mummy?" He stared round, his thumb in his mouth.

The girl Dora sighed, "No, dear, Mummy's gone visiting. She'll be back in time for lunch."

Papa Rookmaaker was often away too. Since the beginning of the century, a programme of decentralisation had been wished onto the native Indonesians. After living under colonial overlords, the idea of having village governments run by native headmen sounded too good to be true, and that is what it turned out to be. The decentralisation programme became a way of saying to the natives, "Let me help you; let me show you how to do it; let me do it for you." The promise of national responsibility only became theirs after World War II, when the Indonesians took it by force. Throughout the twenties, the responsibilities of administering European bureaucracy in an eastern country kept Papa Rookmaaker away from home for weeks at a time, but there were pleasures as well as business.

One day Henderik patted his young son on the head and announced to his family that he was going away to Florus Island for a hunting trip.

"What are you hunting this time, Papa?" one of his daughters wanted to know.

"Dragons."

In 1927, Henderik and a couple of hundred men scoured a Florus valley with ropes and sticks. They caught twelve Komodo Dragons, ten-foot long creatures like leathery lizards with baleful eyes. The ones that survived capture and transportation to Ende harbour were sent to zoos in Amsterdam, Rotterdam, Berlin and London.

The small son of the Resident learned how the seasons changed in Sumatra. The blazing summer turned into the wet season, equally hot. He adjusted to the temperature easily, basking in the warm air. Throughout his life he loathed being cold with the deep, disdainful loathing of a domestic cat.

Whenever Papa came home, it was a happy day with the children running to meet him and the smallest calling the perennial complaint of the youngest in the family, "Wait for me!" Mummy always turned up in time for meals.

Hans learned to call for the people who were nearby when he wanted the needs of childhood satisfied. There was Hennie, and especially there was Dora, the sister he was to say had become like a mother to him. If both girls were out playing tennis there was someone or other from the kitchen at the back of the house who would come running. "Yes, Hansje; see, Mata's here. What you want, my little one? Come then. Something nice for the Son of the Resident. You come with Mata. You see."

Sitting in her Den Haag apartment, the woman Dora looked back half a century to the bright days of her brother's childhood. "Oh, yes, he was spoiled; spoiled by everyone." She pointed to a photo, brown and curled at the edges, brittle as memory, lasting as a dream, "Look, there he is."

There was the four-year-old boy, squatting on the ground eating rice out of a big bowl with his hands. However was the Son of the Resident allowed to do that? Just because he wanted to.

As an older child he was photographed in the wide-legged shorts that children wore in the 1930s, holding a pet monkey on a lead. Pictured on another page, he is holding a mean-looking striped cat perched on his shoulder.

"Tiger cat," said Dora. "They were nice pets but they could not be made clean for the house. We had also a tiger as a pet," she added casually, turning the page.

Indonesians from the nearby plantation had killed the mother tiger and had brought the cub to the Resident's Palace to amuse the children. They had fed it with a baby bottle, and it had played about the house like a huge kitten. It scratched the expensive rugs and was restrained by a lead. Hans, Hennie and Dora pampered it for three months till it was judged to be too big for safety and was dispatched, well humanised, to the Zoo. Another childhood pet was a bear cub that came to the Palace the same way and also departed a few months later in the direction of the Zoo.

Having pets like these was as normal as having a puppy, though there could be problems. A monkey's instinctive terror of tigers affects a monkey's bowels. If you happen to brush past a tiger's fur when you are carrying a monkey the result of that terror can be messy, as Hennie once found to her cost. But there were plenty of servants to clean up. Indeed, the Rookmaaker's servant problem was unusual: there were too many of them.

"What's the matter with Hansje?"

"I told him to pick up his toys. It's not good for the child, Theodora; everyone says Yes, Yes, to him all day long. You spoil him, the servants spoil him, the girls don't leave him anything to do by himself. The child must learn to stand on his own two feet. Oh, Hennie, did you hang up your tennis racket as I told you?"

"It doesn't matter, Papa; Nissan will do it."

"No, Nissan will not do it! You learn to do it! I'm glad we're going back to Den Haag again where you will all have to shift for yourselves!"

Yes, back again. At five and a half years old, Hans was back in Den Haag with his family. At seven years old he was in Atjeh, northern Sumatra, this time with his mother only, while Papa stayed in the Netherlands and the two girls went to High School. At nine, he was back in Den Haag, living in 77 Galvanstraat. It was a cosy house, with living and dining rooms opening out from each other front to back in the Dutch manner. There was a tiny garden at the back and a front door that opened directly onto the street, and dunes just across the road. Hennie and Dora went to Galvanischool, a few doors away; a dark-brick, elaborate building showing a tendency, as with English late-Victorian schools, to look like a cathedral in disguise.

Hans was allowed to spread his belongings about in the dining room. Hennie remembers how one day he had his train-set in an elaborate lay-out all over the floor. According to his small fantasy world, everything was exactly in place. But not according to Theodora. While Hans was outside, she tidied all his dreams away, as mothers are prone to do.

The child returned and wept. "Mummy, how could you have done it! Just when I had it all so *gezellig*!" There is no English equivalent for that splendid word. The nearest translation is 'cosy', but it means much more. *Gezellig* embraces all the rightness and proper-placeness of things; it is the way we feel about the world inside our own front door.

About this time Hans was photographed in the uniform of the *Welpen* (Cubs); a solemn looking child, maybe wondering when his family was going to start packing again. He didn't have to wait long. At thirteen the *Welp* who never graduated to camping with the *Verkenner* (Scouts), was back in the Indonesian jungle, hunting rhinos with his father.

There was no continuity in his environment. Every two years or so he looked out of a different set of windows, learned the names of a different set of servants, attended a different school and played in yet another new neighbour-hood. People react to this kind of childhood in various ways; some thrive, others survive. As a child on the move, Hans learned to put down quick shallow roots, like the American tumbleweed rolling across the prairie. As the diplomat's son, he learned to develop an armour of self-esteem to protect himself from feeling too much the stranger.

One day in Sumatra there was a clash of interests and a clash of family wills. Children from a couple of nearby diplomatic families had arrived to have a swimming tournament in the Rookmaaker pool and Papa Rookmaaker was due to go out hunting. Hans wanted to be in two places at once.

Dora saw him leave the house. "Going hunting after all? It's a pity you aren't swimming this time; you'd be sure to win." Hans had learned to swim at five years old and he swam well. In later life his shoulder muscles would sag and thicken into a scholar's stoop. As a child and adolescent he sliced through the sparkling water like a porpoise.

"I'll be back."

"But the tournament will be over by then, silly."

He tossed his head, "They will wait for me. They have to wait. I'm the Son of the Resident."

"What?" Dora flew down the marble steps, ready to box his ears. "You don't make your friends wait for you one minute! You have to do one thing now or you have to do another thing now—you choose! Son of the Resident indeed!"

He scuffed his high-topped hunting boot along the ground, then his brown eyes came slowly up to meet hers. "OK. I'll swim." He trotted back towards the house flinging a parting shot over his shoulder, "You can tell them they needn't wait for me after all."

Dora, fuming, vowed she would tell them no such thing.

By this time Hans was attending a boarding school on another Indonesian Island, a day's boat ride away from his home. But in his fourteenth year the family was packing again for the boat trip of several weeks, back to the Netherlands.

This time Henderik Rookmaaker looked wistfully over the ship's rail as the green slopes of Sumatra faded to a line on the horizon. He doubted he would ever see the country again. It would be all memories now: the vivid grass on the hillsides and the rice paddies gleaming in the evening light, the sway-backed roofs of native houses, the air marinated in spices, and the *betjak* bicycle-rickshaws trundling along the streets of the town.

A mild heart attack had forced the Resident into retirement at the age of forty-nine. Latterly there had been puzzling signs of unrest among the nationals but Henderik felt he had done his best for them for a quarter of a century. Before he left, a frog had been named after him.

He had helped a Frankfurt herpetologist catch nineteen specimens of the amphibian in the same year he had gone hunting Dragons. As the ship pulled away from the ex-Resident's beloved islands, he knew his name would remain there, borne by a dark-brown, narrow-mouthed, foot-long denizen of the rain forest: *Oreophryne rookmaakeri Mertens*. (Mertens was the herpetologist.)

Back in the Netherlands, the Rookmaakers unpacked in Ranonkelstraat 17 in north-west Den Haag. They spread themselves and their Indonesian *objets d'art* on three floors and Hennie poured her pounds of unroasted coffee beans into the two-foot high Chinese vase for safe keeping. (It was to come in more useful than she realised at the time.) Henderik began to establish useful business contacts. Dora shook out her dresses and planned to buy new ones. Mevr. Rookmaaker got in touch with her friends and went out right after lunch to go tripping and trolleying all over Den Haag. Hans rejoined the swimming club.

The view from the corner windows of their new home was of trim houses, brick-paved streets and the tops of the trees in Bosjes van Poot park, but there was more to the world than this, as Hans knew from snatches of grown-up conversation. Living in Europe, the activities of the world outside the family circle began to invade his consciousness. In Sumatra there had been the radio and the newspapers, but here there were friends who had been watching recent events for themselves. It was all much closer.

There were some long faces among the adults around the dining table at Ranonkelstraat 17, and there was serious talk with Henderik's friends after dinner. Strange news was filtering across the border from Germany. The year was 1936.

CHAPTER THREE

Storm Clouds

THE NETHERLANDS HAS 994 kilometres of land boundary on the east and south; 544 of those kilometres unite her with Germany, but the ties between the two countries are closer than geography. The Dutch and the Germans are both Saxon people. Their languages are closely linked. When the Dutch sing their National Anthem they begin with the words, "I'm William of Nassau, of German blood." William of Oranje-Nassau, nicknamed William the Silent, was the Dutch national hero who helped unite the Netherlands against sixteenth-century Spain. He was born in Dillenberg, Hesse.

Queen Wilhelmina, whose active reign spanned the eventful years from 1898 to 1948, married Henry, Duke of Mecklenburg-Schwerin, another German. In 1936 her daughter, then Princess Juliana, married the German Prince Bernhard of Lippe Biesterfeld. The royal house of Oranje-Nassau has connections with Germany as naturally as the House of Windsor has connections with Scotland. Among the commoners, Dutch-German marriages along the western 544 kilometres made the threat of hostilities with Germany seem like the threat of civil war.

The adult conversations Hans Rookmaaker heard in his teen years were increasingly about the troubles on the other side of the border.

"They'll respect our neutrality, you'll see. Pass the port, Henderik."

"No, don't listen to him. I tell you, Henderik, ever since the Reichstag fire they've had trouble brewing over there. That was on your eleventh birthday, young Hans, but you wouldn't remember the stir the news caused. I think you were all in Sumatra then. They said van der Lubbe started the fire because he was Communist; now dear knows when civil liberties will be restored. It's bad for business; I've seen the effects for the last three years."

"Well, I still say you're making too much of a little thing. Henderik's seen unrest in Indonesia. It all blows over, doesn't it?"

"I don't know. Sometimes." It had seemed in moments of fearful imagination as if a death-wish had seized the colonial administration. Maybe they had been digging their own graves there for three hundred years. Henderik drew on his cigar and listened to his friends talk politics. It seemed in those days that everyone in Europe was talking politics.

New administrations and political parties had been springing up overnight in the fresh green grass of post-Kaiser Germany. It was hard to tell the innocuous from the poisonous; hard to predict which party would shrivel in a matter of months and which would survive. The new youth movement in the next door country seemed quite whole-some now; members attended Lutheran church in their brown-shirted uniforms. They acquired a friendly nick-name: the Nazis.

From time to time there was a violent incident directed against German Jews. But anti-Semitism had been around for centuries, and every movement has its undisciplined members, said the Rookmaaker elders, rustling their daily copy of *Algemeen Handelsblad*. It was just a case of the Nazi theme of German race purity getting a little out of hand.

While all this was going on beyond the boundary line, Hans was involved in school. His education had happened in bits and pieces; a year or two in Den Haag, then a year or two on the other side of the world with new books, class-rooms, teachers and ways of learning. Hans was a sur-prising child. He responded to the upheaval by learning well.

At eleven he had done all the work required for twelve-year-olds, the age when High School begins. School reports had been delivered to the Rookmaaker home at the end of every term and they were consistently good. His parents had great hopes for their son.

"High School a year early," breathed his mother. "My clever boy!"

"My brother," announced Hennie, "has a brain like a sponge."

But at the end of that school year, 1933, the letter from the Headmaster was frank. "Mentally he is ready for High School. He can do the work. But in himself he is not ready for it at eleven years. Let him do the last year again and move up at the proper time."

Theodora was furious, but it didn't matter because they were due to leave for Indonesia that summer. Hans was put into High School in Indonesia a year ahead of his age. (That was when he was boarded out, returning home for the holidays by boat to his parents' island.) It turned out that the Den Haag Headmaster had known best after all; that year was the only time Hans failed an exam.

At twelve, Netherlands children have a choice: they go to Technical High School for five years, or Gymnasium for six years. The Gymnasium includes Latin and Greek. With the full agreement of his parents, Hans chose the five-year course at Technical High School. It had more maths. The world of arts and classical languages had no interest for him then.

Childhood came to its inevitable end with a deepening voice and outgrown clothes. Hans shot up to medium height and stayed there, filling out round the middle. He inherited the plumpness of his later life from the distaff side of the family. His strong nose was more evident in profile at this time than in adult photographs, when his cheeks had rounded and sagged with maturity. His brown hair was cut close about the ears in the fashion of the 1930s. He had limpid brown eyes and an impish grin that wandered up one side of his face. His close nature earned him some teasing from schoolmates but his courtly manners made him popular with the High School girls.

He had been sent to a Christian, that is a Reformed, High School; not an unusual establishment in the Netherlands where the traditional ties of religion and education are still close. He was sent there because it had a good standard.

An intelligent and silent child, Hans noticed a lot and evaluated what he saw. To some people in that school, the name Christian was nothing but a decorative fringe added onto the stuff of life, but to others it seemed to be the warp threads of the fabric itself. Young Hans noticed the difference. He liked what he saw. He mentioned it to Dora: "They're different; I'd like to be like them."

But at the time she paid little heed. This young lady had other things on her mind. Her silly young brother disappeared into his room to play jazz records while Dora combed her hair and listened for the doorbell.

Hans' sisters were pretty after the fashion of their time, with short, crimped hair, white shoes and stockings and pale summer dresses cut wide about the hips; a style designed to make every young lady look pearshaped. Their mother kept wandering in and out of their days, tasting coffee here, tea there and cream cakes everywhere; the life and soul of other people's parlours. She was the way she had been throughout her son's life. But now there were changes in Hans' family.

"Doortje?"

"She's out," said Hennie, "Off with that boy again. What do you want, Hansje?"

As he passed through adolescence, it was sister Hennie who sewed on Hans' buttons and searched through his drawer for a spare shoelace, while Dora spent more and more time with the Haver Droese boy they had all known since their early schooldays.

Maybe Hans was sad when she married him but Dora snorted at the suggestion years later: "I already told you, he never said his feelings—not even to me. But yes, I think he missed me."

Dora went with her new husband to Indonesia, the third generation of her family in the colonial civil service.

"You'll be glad to get away from the awful news from Germany," friends said when they came to the house to wish the young couple goodbye.

35

"Oh, it will blow over. What I am glad to get away from is Hans' jazz records playing next to my room all day and all night!"

"Oh, Doortje!"

"Yes, you and your 'Oh, Doortje'! You claim you are studying and all I hear is Boomp, Boompety, Boomp!"

"Oh, Doortje!"

"Hah! By the time I come back in two years, you'll have outgrown jazz, I hope!"

But he never did. One day for ten cents, he had impulse-bought a 78 of Jelly-Roll Morton. He had played it to himself, played it to his friends, played it to his sisters till everyone in Ranonkelstraat 17 knew it by heart. Hans claimed you could understand a record better the more times you played it.

"I think," Dora remembered, "he played that record till it was quite smooth and we were all ready to scream. After three months he swapped it for a friend's record. It was American Negro jazz again."

There was a lot of the 1920s in the music then: stop-time and bluesy brass, a persistent undertone of speakeasy creak. Jelly-Roll Morton was playing with the *Red Hot Peppers*, cutting records of *Doctor Jazz* and *Smoke-House Blues*. The music demands that you take it seriously, then laughs in your face when you do. It has bold campy wit, it has style; for some reason the sound reached out to young Hans and never let him go.

Soon every guilder of his pocket money was being spent on records and needles. He saved up to buy, he swopped, he borrowed. He and friends from High School lolled about in his room in the way of fast-growing, always-tired teenage boys, while drumbeats drifted through the open windows into the sunshine of Hans Rookmaaker's fifteenth summer.

Across the border in Germany, things were throbbing to the beat of a different drum. As inflation turned the cash foundations of society into a quicksand, the Germans were so tired of revolutions and weak governments that they were ready for any leader who could promise them solid ground. Old regimes were gone and their house was swept and empty. Their new leader might have been an example of

Germanic greatness; he might have been a saint. In the inscrutable plan of God, the leader they chose was Hitler.

In 1933 civil liberties were suspended; the first concentration camp was built in Bavaria, in a little place called Dachau. In March, a German newspaper reported that it had room for five thousand political prisoners. By the summer of 1933 the Vatican had become sufficiently concerned for the safety and religious freedom of German Catholics that it drew up a concordat with National Socialist Germany. Next year the Hitler Youth Movement took over most other youth organisations, including those run by churches. The days of public Lutheran church attendance by young Nazis were over. People in the Netherlands became worried.

The Lutherans in Germany reacted nervously and in various ways. Theirs was a national church, and the Nazis were nationalistic. It was not easy for the Lutherans to condemn them outright. Some pastors went so far down the anti-Semitic road that they dropped Hebrew words like Hallelujah and Amen from their liturgies, substituting German words. Other pastors spoke courageously but their words went to the wind.

The 1936 Encyclical of Pius XI expressed burning concern over the events in Germany. "Whoever exalts race, or the people, or the State, or a particular form of State, or the depositors of power . . . to an idolatrous level, distorts and perverts an order of the world planned and created by God; he is far from the true faith in God and from the concept of life that faith upholds. . . . The fool who has said in his heart 'There is no God' goes straight to moral corruption and the number of those fools who today are out to sever morality from religion is legion. . . . [To the young] Sing your hymns of freedom, but do not forget the freedom of the children of God."

These were stirring words but the freedom to act on them had been whittled away. A chain of small decisions had been made till the nation was bound by the results. On one side of the border lived Hans and his contemporaries so long trained in habits of tolerance that they could accept a Dutch

Nazi Party without great concern. On the other side of the border were the youth of the New Order, restless as wandering birds, bred upon dreams of steel.

By the time Hans turned sixteen, the German slogan *ein Volk, ein Reich, ein Führer*, had replaced one Church, one Faith, one Lord. Maybe idealism without Christ always goes wrong. Though he was not aware of it at the time, the subject that was to interest him for the rest of his life began to take root in Hans' mind: the question of how God works in history. In the 1970s the grey-haired Hans Rookmaaker was to give a lecture to philosophy and art students in London, saying:

> Man is not just a piece of straw on the flow of history. He can go against the stream. It may mean we are drowned, swallowed, damaged, thrown aside; that we don't come to the end. But it is better to go upstream, fighting against the stream, than to go down and fall into the deep abyss.

God deals with nations, he insisted, just as God deals with individuals, but in the broad sweep of human history individuals are free to choose. Not only free; they are morally responsible for their own lives, no matter which way their nation goes.

> We Christians are to be salting salt in this world. We are to try to redeem culture, even as salt stops decay and gives taste to things. That is the only task we have. If we are put in a prison camp or a concentration camp, we are not allowed to work any more.

He reconsidered his words with a grim smile: "Well, no, maybe we can work, even there."

CHAPTER FOUR

The Storm Breaks

AT SIXTEEN HANS Rookmaaker had no particular idealism to fight for. His childhood had been as soft as clouds; a Haagener courtliness had been instilled gently into his days. If all had gone well, his native stubbornness would have been overlaid with patrician charm to make a third-generation diplomat; a gentleman with no thought in his head beyond a successful career. If all had gone well, God would have had little use for such a man. As far as the kingdom of God was concerned, his life was as barren as a sand-dune.

When his parents turned his mind to choosing a career, Hans said he wanted to be a colonial civil servant. His father hesitated, "No, I don't think so, Hansje."

Hans was surprised, "Why not?"

"Things are changing out there. If you have to leave, you would have to begin training for a new career all over again. And for goodness sake let us agree on something reasonable. Don't be like Hennie, wanting to study horticulture of all things! Such an unsuitable thing for a girl to do. You get into something profitable and lasting, my boy."

As things turned out, Henderik was right about the colonial career. If Hans had followed in his father's footsteps, he would have had to leave for good in 1949 when full independence was proclaimed in Indonesia. Hans turned his back on the thought of a colonial life and chose the Marines instead. His childhood travels had given him a love of the sea and the engineering side of marine life would put his maths to good use. After Technical High School Henderik planned to send him for two years to Marine Officer's School in Den Helder.

It was a natural place for Henderik to send his son. Just as a well-heeled family in Britain would send their fledgling army son to Sandhurst and an American family with the right connections would enrol their boy in West Point, so Hans Rookmaaker was given the best: Den Helder Marine Officer's School. In that swank establishment perched on the north-west curve of Noord-Holland, near the Texel bird sanctuaries, he was to keep company with other sons of gentlemen and be trained for leadership.

Dora and her husband came home for a visit and one of her first questions was about Hans.

"He's going to Den Helder, dear," said Theodora, "but first he's going away to finish High School in Leiden."

"Where is he going to stay?"

"Stay? In Leiden? I don't know, Dora dear; some *pension*, I expect."

"That child? Mother! He's only sixteen! You cannot let him go and live away from home like that!"

"Oh? Why not, dear?"

"You haven't told him anything!"

"Told him what, dear?"

Dora stamped her foot into the expensive carpet, "Anything! He cannot go out into the world like that! There are dangers, there are"—she used a word that still held some content for her generation—*"temptations!* You must talk to him!"

Mevr. Rookmaaker wavered under the stern eyes of her modern married daughter, "Oh, very well, dear. I'll ask your father to say to him . . . er, whatever is necessary."

But Henderik would not. His was the generation that believed sex education was best achieved by a young man being thrown in at the deep end to learn from experience. Theodora was a typical woman of her generation: she did not want to get her feet wet. Dora raged and stormed at them both without result, then took matters into her own hands.

So it was that Hans' sister and brother-in-law sat him down one day and told him the Facts of Life. He took it all quite calmly and asked a few perfectly normal questions.

Dora scribbled the name of a book on a piece of paper and thrust it into his hand. "There, buy that. It will answer any more questions if you have them."

"Thank you, Doortje." He had grown a little pink.

"Here, Hansje, this is money to pay for the book."

"Thank you, Doortje."

She knew better than to ask him outright if he had read the book, or even if he had bought it. He was an honest lad and probably did buy it, though it is just possible that he considered the money better spent on jazz and blues records.

He loved them all: the prancing boogie-woogie's left hand strutting a cake-walk up and down the bass notes; he loved the Louis Armstrong brass, wowing and wailing like a human voice; he loved the blues singer's personal lament. He was spellbound by how each jazz player went his own way with the inexorable drumbeat that held them together. He tuned his ear to the blue notes, Creole-spiced and rough-edged, to the flatted thirds and sevenths that had been dragged in chains from West Africa; to the slides and slurs that were squeezed out under the Jim Crow laws at the turn of his own century. Thoughtful listening prepared his ear and heart in later life for the diverse unity of Bach, but jazz was always his special joy.

Duly armed against temptation by the words of Dora and her husband, Hans left home. From Leiden High School he went to Den Helder where he took to his marine studies like a duck to water. He was photographed in uniform with the other students; half-proud, half-shy, dressed in trousers of a naval cut, a short jacket with close shiny buttons making him look like a page-boy who has not done up his coat, and with a peaked, braided cap flat on his head. At seventeen, he probably felt extremely adult. He looked absurdly young.

During one of Dora's visits home, she and Hennie took it upon themselves to teach their young brother to dance. The house in Ranonkelstraat whooped with shouts and laughter as they trod on each other's toes.

"Oh, Hansje, your feet are so big! Here, try it with Hennie

41

this time. Hold the way I told you, now—slow, slow, quick-quick, slow. Keep going—oh, mind the Chinese vase!"

Somehow the elegant furniture survived. Hans was equipped with skills in two-step, foxtrot and Lindy Hop and was passed by the critical eye of his sisters as good enough to be let loose in the social world without shaming his family. One evening he made use of his new ability.

"Come on, Hennie."

"Come on, where?"

"To that dance I told you about."

"I don't think I want to go. You go."

"No, I've got to have a girl to go with and you'll do."

"Thank you for the gracious invitation, little brother."

"Oh, come on, Hennie; you'll enjoy it when you're there."

Hennie did not know how much her choice involved. "All right, then; I'll go. Give me time to make myself look nice."

There was probably a typical teasing brother's answer to that.

Blending with the other couples in the dance hall, Hans and Hennie moved around the floor, trying the new jitter-bug steps they had practised at home. Dance music in 1939 was played by a live band, usually a piano, violin, bass, saxophone and a discreet set of drums. Much of the dance music was imported from America; Irving Berlin and Cole Porter were familiar names. British tunes to cross the Noordzee included *Lambeth Walk* and *Me and My Gal*.

Halfway through the evening there was a lull. People sat around the dance floor on spindly gold chairs, the boys smoothing their neat hair, the girls repairing powder and lipstick and straightening their stocking seams. When the music began again it was in a softer, more romantic mood.

Young Hans looked across the room, "That's a nice girl. Let's go and meet her."

Hennie thought it was an unusual thing for a shy brother to suggest. She followed his glance, "Which girl? Oh I see, the blonde. All right."

They crossed the dance floor. Boy and girl shook hands,

introducing themselves Dutch-fashion by giving their names.

"Hans Rookmaaker."

"Riekie Spetter."

Hennie got between them somehow and held out her hand. "Hennie Rookmaaker. I'm his sister."

"Will you dance with me, Riekie?" They stepped onto the floor together while Hennie found herself another partner for the rest of the evening.

Something had happened to Hans that night and Hennie described it years later, using a turn of phrase that sounds so odd from a sober Dutch lady that it must be true: "It was love at first sight."

Soon Hans' jazz records were providing music for many good evenings with friends. He and Dik and Marcus, Anky, Riekie and the others got together to listen to jazz. When they grew tired of listening sitting still, they danced; Anky with Marcus, Hans with Riekie, whose blonde head just reached to Hans' shoulder. To look at Riekie, unlike Marcus, no one would have believed she was Jewish.

"Marcus, will your mother let us make coffee again?"

"She said last time we have to tidy the kitchen afterwards!"

"We'll let you do that, since it's your house!"

There was a friendly scuffle and the girls disappeared into the kitchen. (Dutch stomachs are specially adapted for drinking coffee last thing at night.) The boys browsed through Hans' records, the seventy-eights thicker, heavier and more brittle than our familiar LP discs, and each encased in plain brown paper.

Hans wiped a record with his sleeve, set it on the turntable, all thumbs, and then lowered the tone arm gently onto the spinning bakelite. "This one's Billie Holiday. I got it last week; swapped it with a boy I used to know at school."

"What did you swop it for, the Duke Ellington? Oh, she's singing flat!"

"No, she isn't; it's an African musical note. It's like another language. I'll put it on again in a minute. You have to keep listening to understand it."

Chatting over coffee, they planned the next day. The girls wanted to go window shopping. De Bijenkorf's had some of those new blouses with shoulder pads and tiny little buttons. They began to wave their hands, describing them. The boys laughed and groaned and decided to go swimming. They belonged to the same Den Haag swimming club and swam races against each other, often arguing that Hans ought to have a handicap because he won so often.

"Maybe we should tie a bunch of Billie Holiday records to his feet."

"No good; he'd use them like flippers and go even faster."

They made vague plans to drop in at Pieter's house in the evening for bridge.

Finally they broke up for the evening and walked the girls home. Then Hans paced back to Ranonkelstraat, his bundle of records tied up with string. Den Haag was so quiet he could hear the breakers coming in from the Noordzee along the Scheveningen coast.

The unholy German Empire was reaching its crooked claws over Europe and the adults were worried, but for Hans life could still be good. It was a pity he didn't see so much of Hennie now that she had married her economist boy-friend and left the family home. She visited their parents for the occasional weekend. With Hennie and Dora gone, Hans felt a greater gap between himself and his parents.

He let himself in the front door. His mother was still up. She jumped when she heard the key, "Well? Did you have a nice evening? Tell me all about it. Where did you go? Whom did you see?"

"Marcus' house."

"Who else was there? Was Riekie there? What about Dik?"

"Friends."

"What did you do? Did you have supper? I see you took records; did you play them? Which ones did you take?"

"Some of them."

"Yes? That was nice. Where are you going tomorrow? Are you going to be with Marcus?"

"Mm." He moved towards the foot of the stairs.

"Don't make a noise going upstairs, dear. Papa hasn't been sleeping well. He's worried about, er . . . things."

Hans slipped his shoes off in the hall and padded his big feet upstairs, holding his records close to his chest like a baby. Mevr. Rookmaaker watched him, trying to push away her concern. Dear God, what would happen to young Marines if war came?

By 1940, when Hans was eighteen, people had become openly concerned about their neighbour country. Many had business and family ties there. The news and rumours grew daily worse. The Dutch are as insular as any proud nation, but they are not an island. Now only 544 kilometres of boundary signposts lay between them and the Third Reich.

By the time Hans took the train from Den Haag to Den Helder for his second year of Officer's School, people's words had shifted subtly from, "England would help us if we were attacked" to "I hope England *will* help us *when*—". Hitler moved into Austria in 1938, into Czechoslovakia and Poland in 1938 and '39, and the unthinkable became the inevitable. Hans still heard some adults speaking hopefully about their policy of independence but most knew that war with Germany was only a matter of time.

It came with the dawn of Whitsun, May 10th 1940. "Henderik! Henderik! Wake up at once!"

". . . hmm . . ."

"Henderik, wake up! What's that strange noise? It sounds like banging over the coast! And that's a plane going over low! Henderik, what is it?"

"Hm? Huh? Ssh, I want to listen." He stumbled out of bed and groped his way to the window.

"Henderik, why are all those people in the street at this hour? It's barely past four a.m.!"

Her husband leaned from the open window and hailed a man in the street. "What's going on?"

The man was struggling into an overcoat over his pyjamas. He called back, "Planes—bombing—parachutes! They are bombing the harbours and the airfield! They are attacking us!"

45

"Who is bombing us? We are neutral! You must have got it wrong, my friend!"

"No," said another, shivering in bare feet on the paving stones, "it is they who are wrong, the Germans. They are more wrong than you can think. They have attacked us!"

"Papa, Mummy, are you awake?" Hennie's voice came through the bedroom door, "Hansje will be sorry to be away in Den Helder tonight. I'll finish dressing and go outside to find out more."

"Oh, Hennie dear, be careful!"

"Theodora, we'll all go out. It seems the world and his wife are walking about in the streets tonight."

May 10th 1940 should have been a glorious dawn. The sky over Den Haag glowed like a pearl, the air was fresh and crisp from the Noordzee. But this morning the gulls were silent and the open dome of heaven was ripped across by vicious dark planes that chased and dived and wheeled and spat. With the familiar uncoordination of lightning and thunder, the flash of fire was followed half a second later by the noise of shell-burst.

A group of people began cheering, "That's one of ours, the ones with the orange markings! We're being defended! Long live the Netherlands! Oranje above all!"

Another group took up the cry of hope with the National Anthem, the long musical phrases of the sixteenth-century tune pressing forward like a breaker surging against the dunes, *"Wilhelmus van Nassouwen ben ick van Duytschen bloedt . . ."*

The sound seemed thin and out of place sung on a street corner in the thin cold dawn. Up in the sky, other men of German blood were busily eliminating the defence of the Dutch airforce. It had been no more than a small swarm of midges in the face of an eagle.

Adults with memories that could reach back twenty years, could remember the Great War. "They left us alone then; they respected neutrality." One man propped his radio on the front window-sill and a silent group was clustered near it, families with their arms round each other's shoulders. "But we are neutral . . . that is, we *were* neutral.

How could they do this to us? Something terrible has happened when a nation does not keep its word."

As the light of May 10th grew, the darkness of the facts closed round them. The German planes that had been seen roaring overhead towards England had turned round over the Noordzee and headed back to bomb the airfields. While parachutists were landing around Den Haag to seize the Queen and the Government, Nazi troops with tanks were crossing the border from the east.

Hennie, Henderik and Theodora wandered the streets of their neighbourhood for a while, listening to comments, greeting friends, voicing their shock and concern. The sky grew lighter till it was almost to be called day rather than night. All at once, people became aware that they were out in public in their nightclothes. Sheepishly they filtered back to their homes, letting themselves in with a feeling of chill unreality. It was too early for breakfast, too late to call it night.

Some brewed coffee and sat around the kitchen stove; some fled back to their tepid beds and tried to blot out the world for two or three hours of ordinary sleep. Those who could, prayed. Children fell asleep at last, dreaming of how they alone would breach the *dijk* in the path of invading armies, crawl through the flak with the crucial secret code, or stand against all odds to face the Nazis, armed only with a toy pistol and the might of a loyal Netherlander.

Hans Rookmaaker was no longer a child. When the news was broken, grim-faced, to the Marine Midshipmen at breakfast in Den Helder, Hans drew his thoughts tightly round his head like a blanket. He knew only one thing for certain: that the world he had awoken to that morning would never be the same.

CHAPTER FIVE

"The Oranje Hotel"

AT EIGHT A.M. a very angry Queen Wilhelmina broadcast to her people, making "a flaming protest against this unprecedented violation of all good faith, and violation of all that is decent between cultured states. I and my Government will do our duty. Do your duty everywhere and in all circumstances. Every man to his post."

Families stood to attention for the playing of *The Wilhelmus*; the younger children wide-eyed and silent, the older ones covering fear with bravado, the adults grim-faced with tears of rage in their eyes. Hans, if possible, became more indrawn than usual. His Marine School training had acquired a nasty purposefulness.

It was a miserable Friday. People did not know enough to make long-term plans, but they knew too much to behave normally. The effects of the disturbed night had left some of them ragged. Many went to work but did no work to speak of; conjecture filled the day and everyone's radio was left on in hope of news. Other cities had been attacked and two bombers had been brought down in the centre of Den Haag. Suddenly it seemed as though Nazi soldiers were everywhere. One day there had been no sign of them; the next day the land was swarming with them. It was almost as if they had been coming in for weeks, disguised in other clothes and hidden in canal barges. They had.

That Saturday people shopped and ate meals in a daze. That Sunday the churches were more full than usual. Many felt the support of the Christian faith, or rediscovered it, or went to look for it. It is not recorded how the Rookmaakers spent the day.

On Monday 13th the nation felt an additional stab of

sorrow; this time a sorrow like that of bereavement. "No, no, it is not true!" "Yes, it was on the radio; the Queen has left us. She is on her way to England. We are alone."

Later they understood the wisdom of the move that took the Queen, her family and her Government into exile to continue the fight. At the time, the nation felt bewildered and bitter. The British destroyer, *Hereward*, brought the sixty-year-old Queen to England on the day that Churchill was telling the House of Commons that he had nothing to offer his own country but "blood, toil, tears and sweat".

Meanwhile the Dutch army continued to sweat out what fight was left. It was no use. On May 14th a squadron of bombers unloosed their terror raid on the streets of Rotterdam. At one thirty in the early afternoon, Heinkels dive-bombed the densely populated area near the station.

"A splendid picture of invincible strength," remarked a Nazi observing the planes roaring low over the city. In fact, it had as much nobility as an act of rape. The town was undefended and unprepared. Hospitals, churches and thousands of houses were reduced to a horror landscape of shattered brick. Whole blocks of homes were flattened as though by a giant roller. Four days later the Dutch began plans to rebuild the city.

The Nazis claimed that only three hundred lives were lost, though the Dutch were still digging bodies out of the wreckage three weeks after the attack. With gallows humour, a Rotterdam clergyman prayed at a memorial service, "I commemorate the three hundred dead in our city, of whom eight hundred fell in my parish alone."

Hans Rookmaaker's little neutral country sounded the ceasefire and a dreadful silence hung over the streets of the Netherlands.

"Hans, I am afraid!" Riekie's blue eyes were wide in her pale face. "What will they do to us? Will it be like Crystal Night? Oh, Hans, what will happen to us now?"

"Don't worry, Riekie, you'll see, it will be all right." The meaningless but inevitable words were spoken many times to many Jewish friends throughout the country. The Dutch could not bring themselves to believe that the barbarities they had heard about in news from Germany could happen within their own nation.

The Netherlands has had a long history of toleration; they like to think for themselves and admire others who do the same. Once upon a time anti-semitism was almost regarded as one of the Christian virtues, but when the old medieval order of life changed and people were looking for new identities and authority, the Netherlands became the sanctuary of Europe for persecuted believers. Lutherans, Calvinists, Catholics and Jews were made to feel equally at home in the little delta land. They brought their skills with them and helped to bring about the Golden Age.

But now the Dutch were no longer their own masters. The chief man of the country was the bespectacled lawyer Artur Seyss-Inquart, the quisling of Vienna. As Gauleiter of the occupied Netherlands, he might do anything.

"I'm afraid, Hans. We're not allowed to mention pogroms at home for fear of frightening my young brother. But he knows, of course; we all do."

There was only one comforting thought, but Hans dared not put it into words. Riekie did not look Jewish, so if the worst came to the worst, she would probably be all right. He underestimated the thoroughness of the Nazi race-detection laws.

At first Seyss-Inquart spoke softly to his occupied land, telling the people on May 29th: "As Reich commissioner I shall exercise the supreme command in civic affairs over the Dutch citizens, protected by the German arms, to maintain law and order. I shall take all necessary steps, eventually by decree, to complete this task. In doing so, I wish, as much as possible, to respect the Dutch law and independent jurisdiction, as well as to consult the Dutch authorities. And I expect all judges, public administrators and civil servants rigorously to enforce my laws."

The Rookmaakers read the published statement with mixed feelings. As a civil servant, Hans' father could be in a tricky position. As things turned out, he was free to continue his life as retired colonial Resident. He filled in the required form, declaring himself not of Jewish extraction. His diplomacy stood him in good stead and he managed to give both sides the impression of being friendly. But within a few days of Occupation, the presence of the armies was felt.

"It's disgraceful! Do you know there is not one pair of silk stockings in the whole of Den Haag!" Theodora reeled off a short list of friends who had been having a similar shopping problem. "Not a single pair, I tell you! And as for scented soap, you might as well be asking the shop assistant for green diamonds!"

Silk stockings and good soap had vanished from the face of the Dutch earth. So had luxury lingerie, chocolate, jewellery and ladies' watches. The Nazi soldiery had descended like locusts, stripping the Dutch shelves bare to clothe and pamper their wives and girl-friends at home. Because of the relative economies of the two countries, Germans could buy cheaply when the price ticket was marked in Dutch guilders. In a crowded shop, anyone in Nazi uniform immediately went to the head of the queue, arrogantly acting out the saying, "The human race begins with the rank of lieutenant."

The Nazis had convinced themselves that they were better at anything than any other nation on earth. Hard on the heels of the invading soldiers came an army of bureaucrats, taking over everything that involved paperwork and making paperwork where there had been none before. They even sent representatives of the glorious Reich into Friesland to teach the Dutch how to breed cows.

As weeks of occupation passed into months, there were signs that Seyss-Inquart's newly captured people were not altogether enchanted with the idea of being absorbed into the Third Reich. Nazi soldiers patrolling the streets of Amsterdam and Den Haag at night found the hard way that they had to go in twos. A single soldier was a target for trouble. The darkened street would seem empty; just the flicker of a breeze on water, leaf-fall and an occasional cat. Then sudden footsteps, a quick shove and the street would ring with the curses of a Nazi soldier trying to empty mud out of his rifle. Young Dutchmen had discovered a new use for their canals.

If a uniformed Nazi was unwise enough to walk the streets alone and drunk, he would be found in the canal next morning, floating face down. If a German spy was captured, he immediately claimed to be Dutch, but loyal Netherlanders had a foolproof way of testing nationality; they learnt it from the Shibboleth test in the *Book of Judges*. The man was asked, at gun-point, to pronounce the name of the Den Haag sea-side resort, Scheveningen. If he pronounced it wrong, his life was short.

Nazi reprisals were so vicious that Dutch stubbornness grew stronger. Soon concentration camps had to be built at Vucht and Amersfoort, each designed to hold twenty thousand. Still the nation was not to be cowed. "The Germans have invaded Dutch territory," said Queen Wilhelmina, "but they have not invaded Dutch spirit."

Hans and his friends were free to go on with their lives as before; chatting over coffee, playing jazz and going swimming. The Marine School had been closed down and Hans was transferred to the Den Haag Technical High School for a course in engineering.

The harsh anti-semitic laws were to come in a little later. For the first period of occupation, the Jews were left alone, except that their identity cards were stamped across with the letter J. Being singled out by Nazi officialdom was worrying. Why did their cards need to be distinguished from those of their Gentile neighbours? Riekie, Marcus and the others looked worried and spoke of Crystal Night, but Gentile friends assured them, "It can't happen here."

"There are thousands of Jews living in this country. What would the Nazis gain by going against them all? Anyway, Marcus, they won't hurt you since your father makes their uniforms now."

He hung his dark head, "We're not working with them, you know. They're just new customers, nothing more. If my father ran a baker's shop, should he refuse to sell them bread?"

It was the kind of question they all had to face in one way

or another. The Underground papers fulminated against collaborators as though there was no moral distinction between selling a loaf of bread to a Nazi soldier and selling a hundred countrymen by an act of betrayal. Men in business and administration were in difficult positions. Some chose to go one way, some another. There were not enough clear-cut moral guidelines to make any of them feel at ease.

At the age when students like to sit around theorising about right and wrong, Hans Rookmaaker was brought face to face with how hard it is to draw the line in practice. Others talked and argued; he sat listening. In later years he was seen to have a rare understanding in counselling students. Though he never watered down the strength of truth, he never underestimated the complexities of real life. But in those days, counselling students was the last thing in his mind.

Having believed absurdities, the men of the Third Reich committed atrocities. In the occupied Netherlands the atrocities began slowly. At first they were only rumours to toy with before the young people made coffee and learned new jitterbug steps. (The Lindy Hop was called the jitterbug now.) After a while the rumours became a subject to avoid. People had begun to disappear.

Nearer to the end of the war, Marcus was one of them. In 1944 he was ordered to report to the Jewish Council and everyone feared the worst. But he was back among them next day. "What happened?" They crowded round. "Oh, nothing much, just a warning to behave."

Then he was called to report again. But again he came bouncing home the following day, "Cat and mouse game. Such silly people." There seemed no logic to the way the Nazis behaved. Marcus was ordered to report a third time. He waved goodbye to Anky and went off grinning. "It doesn't bother me. Cat and mouse." She never saw him again.

Years later she spoke of him in the sparce words of someone who has come to terms with a long-ago loss. "We heard later through the Red Cross. The Germans took him to Bergen-Belsen and he died there from no food."

When Hans was still in Den Haag at the beginning of the Occupation, people were disappearing by the razzia, the Nazi version of the Press Gang. Young men of likely age were snatched from the streets or trams and carried off to work in German munitions factories till they died. Everyday life acquired a nightmare quality in which it was not safe to send a teenage son out to post a letter because the razzia might snatch him away for ever. Hans and his circle of special friends numbered eight. Only four of them survived the war.

Apart from the razzia, people began to disappear more deliberately. Like Anne Frank and her family in Amsterdam, many people went underground. The name for them was *onderduikers*, those who dive for cover. "It is only by diving under," said the Dutch, "that you can keep your head above water."

Some of the rumours in Hans' circle were about events uncomfortably near to Den Haag. Reports were filtering in about the prison at Scheveningen where Nazis held people without trial for months. It seemed that there was no pattern of justice in Scheveningen prison; treatment of the prisoners depended on the whim of the guards. Outside the building, prisoners were executed on the windblown dunes. The last thing many a loyal Dutchman saw of this earth was the seagulls wheeling above the trees in the.park, and the last sound he heard was the sigh of breakers driving in from the Noordzee. The Dutch named the Scheveningen prison "The Oranje Hotel".

Until March 1942, when the Japanese took over the Dutch East Indies, Hans managed to keep up a correspondence with Dora who was in a Nazi-inspired internment camp in Java. After the coming of the Japanese, letters and other Red Cross activities were brought to a stop, but for a valuable while the young brother and older sister shared small pieces of their separated lives, with Dora giving Hans good advice in his growing love for Riekie. A familiar post-script from Dora read, "But don't show this to Mummy!" As usual, Hans showed very little to anyone.

His close nature made him seem a natural choice for

Resistance work. People were watching and wondering if the son of the Den Haag diplomat would like to get involved in the Underground. Hans was never formally involved, but his slight contact with the Underground Press proved to be one of the turning points of his life.

The Nazis had landed in the Netherlands on May 10th 1940. The first Underground paper appeared on May 18th. Distribution was the public part of the system and distributors were chosen with care. Street numbers had to be memorised instead of written down. Before long there were reports of distributors who were picked up and tortured till they revealed the names and addresses of everyone else.

Besides the more solid newspapers, there were single news sheets mimeographed or typed or handwritten. They were circulated among University students in the manner of Russian Samizdat literature. It was some of these mimeographed sheets that were offered to Hans for distribution one evening; they bore photos of the Queen.

After visiting friends, his host drew him aside. "Which way are you going home from here?"

Hans told him.

"Care to distribute some papers for us? You can memorise the addresses in a couple of minutes. They are all on your way home."

Yes, he would do it.

The papers were counted out and folded small. Was he sure of the street numbers? Yes, he was sure.

"Be careful, then. Good luck. Oranje above all."

Hans walked out into the twilight. It would be an easy job; he would be home in less than an hour. Maybe he was not careful enough looking up and down the street before he slipped the papers through the letter boxes, or maybe he was too obviously careful. A Nazi soldier stepped out of the shadow of a deep doorway, drawing his pistol.

"Stop! Turn out your pockets!"

Hans tossed his belongings onto the small square paving stones: some money that winked in the street light as it fell; keys, matches, a photo of himself and Riekie sitting on a garden seat, smiling into one another's eyes. The Nazi was only interested in the folded sheets of paper. He snapped his fingers, "Give!"

Hans handed them over, sick at heart. The foliage of a tree nodded in a spring breeze from the nearby coast. People on foot and on bicycles hurried past, made incurious by daily horrors in a world they could not control. A young man was being stopped and searched; there was nothing they could do.

"Put your hands on your head. Walk in front of me. *Raus!*"

In occupied Holland there was only one way of dealing with loyal Dutch who were caught working for the Underground Press. A bullet was put through the heart, and on payment of ten florins, the family was allowed to take the ashes away.

At the Police Station the Nazis took Hans' name and address then bundled him into a car. As he was driven swiftly through Den Haag, he craned his head to read the street signs: Laan van Meerdevoort . . . Stadhouders Laan. They were going past the Zorghvliet Park where Jacob Cats, a poet of the Golden Age, once created a garden from a barren sand-dune. His poem "Zorghvliet" tells of the bare ground that must be tested to see if it will be fruitful.

> I got myself a little piece of land
> To learn by practice what to plant,
> And sandy though it now may be, this dune,
> These white hills are going to bloom;
> Trees of all kinds I intend to plant,
> To try the strength of this piece of sand.

Hans asked the Nazi what he feared he already knew. "Where are you taking me?"

"The Oranje Hotel."

CHAPTER SIX

A Virgin Bible

AT LAST THE post came to the Spetters' house and Riekie grabbed the Red Cross letter-form out of her mother's hand.

"I know who that's from!" Her young brother spread margarine on his bread and ate it plain. These days there was no *chocolade-hagel* to shake over buttered bread for the favourite Dutch breakfast treat.

"Don't tease so," his mother said, "Hans is a nice boy, a good boy and from a fine family. What's the news from prison, Riekie?"

"Oh! Ooh! Oof! That Hans!"

"It's good news?"

"It's *nothing* news!"

"You're not happy with what he tells you, Riekie?" Her father looked up from his cup of wartime coffee.

"I'm—ooh! I don't know whether to laugh or scream! There—there's the letter; read it for yourself while I get my coat. I'm going to share this with Anky Huitker."

Minutes later she stood on her friend's doorstep, the early summer sun lighting her hair, "I got a letter from Hans."

"From Scheveningen? Oh, come in quickly and read it to me! After so many weeks without news, oh, Riekie, I'm glad for you! How is that Hans of yours? They don't let him play jazz records in the Oranje Hotel, I'm sure. Is the food bad? What does he do all day?" She steered the younger girl up the stairs into the front room. "Now, read it to me." She sat down expectantly.

Riekie's blue eyes twinkled and snapped, tipping up at the corners like the eyes of a merry little cat. She held the sheet of prison paper at arm's length and cleared her throat with a flourish.

"It says, 'I am all right. Love. Hans'."

Anky waited. "That's all? No, it cannot be all he said; it cannot! Show me!" She snatched the letter from Riekie's hand. "It *is* all! How could he do that to you!" She looked at the other side of the Red Cross form but there was nothing more than the address.

"That boy!" Riekie exploded, "He makes me so angry sometimes. You ask him questions but he will not speak!"

"That's because his mother asks too many questions."

"His mother—yes. But I'm not his mother!"

The girls put their heads together, staring at the words on the thin page, as if by force of will they could discover more information around or between the lines. But Hans Rookmaaker had been true to character; incarcerated in a Nazi jail for several weeks, he had revealed no more of his personal life or feelings than a Noordzee mussel. Some shy people express themselves freely in a personal diary. Not him. Only once did his feelings flow out in a letter, but that was later and it was to Dora.

"I know the prison letters are censored," Riekie wailed in mock despair, "but he could have written much, much more than this!" This quirk of Hans Rookmaaker's character was to annoy many more people during the course of his life.

The Oranje Hotel during the Nazi Occupation was a place of fear and death. Behind the brick wall with its single small doorway and corridors of cells locked by an iron grille was the sound of screams and the thud of whips and truncheons. Shots reverberated against the outside walls and Nazi jackboots paced slowly down the corridor to the cells. Hans knew the name of the man who had handed him the Underground papers, and the numbers of the houses to which he had been delivering them as well. The Nazis had efficient and terrible ways of extracting that information. At nineteen, he knew what it was to fear for his life.

Christian faith would have helped in the situation, but Hans didn't have any then.

The Nazis kept him in solitary confinement for three months. The only thing they allowed him to do was read. The only book they gave him to read was a Bible.

That he was given a Bible was not a miracle. Dutch prison law says that any prisoner who does not find a Bible in his cell has the right to ask for one at any time, day or night. Nazi soldiers were not renowned for keeping the laws of the land they had pirated, but for some reason they kept the law with this young prisoner.

Nearly forty years later, his wife still cannot imagine any human reason why Hans was not executed when he was caught. The fact that he was a diplomat's son would not have made any difference.

Anky remembered: "At the very end of the war, when the Germans knew they were losing, they were a little less quick to shoot people. But in 1940 and 1941 everyone who was working for the Underground papers was shot. Looking back now, I think it was because the Lord had something for him to do. That's the only reason I can think that his life was spared."

Till then the Christian faith had played no practical part in his life. The few committed Christians at his school had intrigued him, but only at a distance. He needed a course of study unhindered by the divisive dogmatics that have plagued and split the Dutch Reformed churches for so long. Unknowingly, the Nazis provided him with the time and the place. The miracle was not the fact that a Bible was placed in his hands, but what he did with it during the lonely, fearful weeks. The miracle (if it is not too strong a word) grew from a blend of situation and response.

For three months the pampered Son of the Resident had nothing to do but read Scripture. He had always been a keen student. This time he had no other books or jazz records to compete for his attention. The result was not an instant conversion but it was a conversion in the proper meaning of the word. The path of his life began to shift to another direction.

Not surprisingly, his Protestant parentage and Reformed schooling coloured the interpretation of the words he read, but it was only a colouring. The Bible began to speak to him directly so it was natural that he should add that experience to the sum of his other influences and follow the tradition

59

that holds the written revelation as the Christian's only authority. But though he remained a convinced Reformed Christian all his life, he had the discernment to see beyond the boundaries and appreciate the other traditions of the Christian Church. In the 1950s and 60s of his ministry, this ecumenical view was rare among Evangelicals.

At the beginning of his conversion Hans Rookmaaker had almost no denominational bias. As a result, he almost succeeded in reading that rarest of all rare books, a virgin Bible.

"This is absolutely insupportable!" announced Henderik, "That boy has been locked up nearly three months and God knows what he's doing. Probably twiddling his thumbs and dreaming of that confounded jass or jazz or whatever the word is." At that time the Rookmaakers had no clue that Hans would ever get out alive. Henderik was a man accustomed to being obeyed. He dug through his pile of useful contacts and unearthed an acquaintance who was manager of a potato flour factory in Noord-Holland. The man was a Nazi. Such friendships could be maintained if both parties worked on tiptoe.

After some humming and hawing the Nazi said, "No promises now, but maybe I can get your son out." Three weeks later Hans came home.

"Confound them! See what they are up to now!" Henderik slammed the bill down on the breakfast table, making the porcelain coffee cups rattle.

"What is the matter, dear?"

"Matter? I'll tell you what, Theodora. Those Nazis sent me a bill. I'm supposed to pay seven and a half florins a day for Hans' board and lodging in the Oranje Hotel. Well, I'm damned if I'll pay them a penny of it!" He sent an explosive letter to the occupying powers at Scheveningen.

A few days later the doorbell rang. Hennie opened the door to see a man with a swastika armband. "Good morning." He spoke Dutch like a Dutchman. "I have come about the bill."

"Bill? Wait a minute, please." Hennie called up the stairs, "Father, it's a man about that bill!"

"Oh, you mean the one we can't afford to pay!" There

was a note of malicious triumph in Henderik's voice, "Right. I'll talk to him. Take him into the back room. The carpet in the front room looks too expensive!"

The Dutch Nazi was only a minor bureaucrat and Henderik Rookmaaker quickly disposed of both him and the bill of nearly seven hundred florins.

When Hans came home, people soon realised something had happened to him; he had acquired a sense of direction even though he stumbled with shyness as he tried to put his new ideas into words. More than to anyone else he talked to Riekie. While the others in his group of friends teased him and waited for him to get back to normal (to social conformity) Riekie knew him best. Her Hans had found an idea to captivate his mind and with it he had found his tongue. When other friends showed little interest he returned into himself, only willing to explain when his listener was willing to learn and think alongside him. What intrigued him was what he had read for himself in the Bible but had never heard before: that God works with the nations of the world and that Jesus Christ is the only way for men to come to God.

His old activities continued: the engineering course at the Technical School in Delft, the daily irritants of the presence of Nazi soldiers and identity cards and rations, mixed with the pleasures of evenings with his steady friends. His time with Riekie was not to be as long as he expected. In 1943 ten thousand reserve officers, non-commissioned officers and soldiers were deported. One of those ten thousand was the young man who had been in Den Helder Marine School. On April 29th, Hans received a letter ordering him to appear at the collecting camp at Breda.

There was no hint that the men were to be taken anywhere else. Many of them expected to be back for the next weekend. The Nazis had said there would be no need to take any luggage. "Only a toothbrush." Teutonic thoroughness found a way of making the men believe they were coming back. "Look, it's all right," Hans told Riekie, "This is the train ticket they sent me to get to Breda. It's a return ticket." In the uncertain days of the Occupation it seemed a bad omen for young sweethearts to spend too long saying goodbye.

The men's tickets were clipped by the guard as the train rolled south, past the shattered wreck of Rotterdam and on to the old town of Breda. At their destination they were checked in and locked in with depressing thoroughness. Only for overnight? Few of them believed it now. Next day they were herded onto trains and transported to Nuremberg where, years later, a series of War Trials would try to balance the events with a semblance of human justice.

They stayed in Nuremberg for the summer, coming to terms with their new identity as prisoners of war. Their diet during that time was described as "a little bit starving". One of Rookmaaker's fellow prisoners remembered: "In the morning they gave us a small square of bread, hard bread. With it we had margarine and cheap jam. In the evening we had a half litre ladleful of what they called stew. Water to drink. Nothing more. There were no Red Cross parcels."

Little by little, the prisoner's personal possessions were bartered for daily food. As hunger increased, values changed and the progression of objects placed in the hands of the Nazi guards showed the growing hardship. First to go were fancy key rings and lighters. Then followed signet rings and watches of varying value and sentiment. Weeks went by and the only thing the prisoners thought about was food; how to haggle for it and which guards gave best value. After a while men began to sell their wedding rings and finally they were driven to prising the gold fillings out of one another's teeth—anything to pay the price of enough food.

Once Hans Rookmaaker had toyed elegantly through a seventeen course Indonesian meal with high diplomats sitting at the table. Now he had to humble himself before the insolent guards and sell his watch to keep from fainting with hunger. He sent an occasional postcard to Riekie telling her what he had read in the Bible.

There was a roll call at seven a.m. when the men turned out to stand in rows in the compound, shuffling into place behind each other in lines of five. The guards went down the lines shouting, *"Fünf–zehn–fünfzehn–"* Often the men had to stand while the process was repeated. "Nazis can't count," the men muttered to one another. They learned to stand close together so if one of them swayed on his feet from weakness, the others could hold him upright. There was another roll call at midday and another at five p.m. Bread and jam was handed out after morning roll call and the ladleful of stew was doled into tin mugs before seven p.m.

Between those times the starving men lay on their wooden bunks that had been built three layers high like shelves against the walls. They had no reserves of strength to do much else. Weeks passed and autumn came.

"These walls are double," someone discovered, "Let's get a bit off the inside and feed the fire." The wood-burning stove in the centre of the hut had had to be stoked up with whatever fuel the prisoners could find, and re-lighted with a match begged from the guard.

Before long they had prised away some of the looser boards from the walls and were crowding round the concentration of heat, poking dry splintered wood into the roaring flames.

"What happens when we've burnt all the inside layer of the hut?" "Burn the outside layer as well. Burn down the whole hut and the Nazis will have to give us something better." "You mean they have to give us something else. What makes you think they've got anything better?"

Some of the men privately wondered if they would be expected to live without any heat at all, or be force-marched through the winter days till they dropped from exhaustion to die in the frozen mud at the side of the road. They had left their homes in late April, some of them without overcoats. Now it was late September. In properly built houses and with decent food they would barely have noticed the slowly falling thermometer. Now there was little else to notice. Day after day the temperature dropped, the night chill lengthened into the daylight hours and the huts were systematically stripped of their inside insulation.

They never had the chance to find out what would have happened if they had burned down the whole hut because, without warning, the men were herded into trains again.

The idea that they were valued future officers was now a thinly-disguised fiction. But at least they were not required to walk. Many prisoners were.

The train took them east, through the Bohemian Forest and on and on for hours and then days; held up from time to time by the mechanical confusions of war, then rumbling on again past towns with names that were increasingly hard to pronounce.

It is tempting to think that Hans' new-found faith was a help to him. In fact, it was so new-found that it may not have made much difference in the hard realities of his life. The twenty-one-year-old man probably sank into himself in dumb misery as the train took him relentlessly further and further from everyone he had loved.

It took him to the Polish Ukraine. It left him with the other men in Stanislau, three kilometres from the foothills of Count Dracula's Carpathian Mountains. Hans' first sight of snow had been during a holiday in Switzerland when he was twelve. Now he was to see enough snow and pine-trees to last him a lifetime.

He hugged his arms about him, his knees bent in the keen Ukrainian wind, and thought hopelessly of the fine quality woollen suits hanging in his wardrobe at home. But the trim streets of Den Haag were a thousand miles away and his only luggage was a toothbrush.

CHAPTER SEVEN

The Yellow Star

RIEKIE SNAPPED OFF the thread and put the needle back in her mother's workbasket. The patch on the front of her coat shone like an ugly beacon. Even her young brother's school-coat had to be labelled the same way. Sooner or later she would have to go outside into the spring day and it was better to begin by going to see a friend. It was lucky the Huitker home was only a short walk away; the use of public transport was forbidden for Jews.

Riekie stood in the hallway to do her hair. The small mirror reflected a heart-shaped face with eyes that were used to laughing though they were not laughing now. Her fine blonde hair belied her Jewish race, but no-one had minded about race till now. Some friends were Jewish and some were Gentiles; it was a matter of tolerant indifference which was which. Tolerance and humaneness were qualities bred up in every Low Countries child.

Now suddenly the Netherlanders were no longer their own masters. People with an alien point of view had taken over her country and in their eyes she was one of the Untermenschen: the Sub-humans.

Riekie lowered her head like a criminal and slipped into the street. She passed a restaurant that had a sign in the window: *"Joden niet gewensht"* (Jews not wanted here). Some streets in Den Haag were signposted *"Voor Joden verboden"* (Forbidden to Jews). Park benches were labelled separately: "Only for Aryans" "Only for Jews". Herr Goebbels, Hitler's PR man, had said, "Effective propaganda need not be logical as long as it foments suspicion, comtempt or hatred."

After a short walk Riekie stood in Anky's doorway, her

head still down, feeling her cheeks hot with shame. On the front of her coat was what she had had to buy from the Nazis for four cents and a textile coupon: a patch of yellow cotton five inches across, shaped like a star and printed with the black word JOOD. The star of David.

"Oh, Riekie, come in, come in. We heard this would happen. But you are with friends now! Come on upstairs. I'll take your coat. There, that's better—oh dear, there's one on your dress too!"

Riekie put her hands to her face. "Anky, I'm so ashamed."

"But why be ashamed?" The older girl steered her into the living room. "You can be afraid to be Jewish maybe, but why be ashamed?"

"They make us feel that way. I never was ashamed before. But they make us feel as though we were not even human." Her chin trembled, "Oh, Anky, what's going to happen to us? If the Nazis decide to burn and smash everything Jewish like they did on Crystal Night all over Germany no one can stop them!"

"It is a terrible thing that they did, labelling you all this way! They are terrible people, those Nazis. You know, we don't even look at them in the street; they are like air to us."

"You don't mind me coming here?" She watched her friend's face. These days every value had to be questioned.

"Of course we don't mind! You'll find all the old friends will still be glad to see you."

"I'm glad of one thing," Riekie's voice was suddenly gentle, "I'm glad Hans is not here to see me this way."

"It wouldn't make any difference to that Hans."

"No, no, of course not, but it would have made him sad. You know, Anky, he was different when he'd come out of the Oranje Hotel. He was more gentle."

But none of Riekie's friends had been much interested in how Hans had changed; they were all too busy waiting for him to change back. He hadn't changed back. Instead, he had been swept off to prison camp with no time to say goodbye.

The girls chatted about Hans and other friends who had

been taken away; exchanging rumours that someone had said camps in Poland were better or worse than camps in Germany, and that food was terribly scarce in Bergen-Belsen. From time to time Riekie's hand stole up to feel the David Star sewn on her dress, the way a tongue probes a painful tooth, unable to leave it alone.

"Forget about it," ordered Anky, "You are with friends now. These things don't matter."

"Hans said so many things about how Jesus was Jewish but was for all people in the world." Riekie felt uncertain she could explain things as he had done.

"Yes, I suppose so," said her friend and Riekie was silent.

After a while, Anky walked home with her, "Just to show you that it really doesn't matter to me what you have to wear." A Nazi soldier stared coldly at them as they turned the corner and the girls strode on, ignoring him and all he stood for.

Finally the Red Cross got confirmation of Hans' arrival at Stanislau POW camp. There was no personal news: just that he was one of those who had arrived and that, at the time of sending the information (several weeks before it reached Den Haag) he had been alive and reasonably well. As Theodora wept, Henderik sagged in his chair; his world was crumbling apart, the pieces shattered and scattered like the rubble of a building that had never been completed. He had had such high hopes for his son. What could the young man make of his life now?

While Hans was away, his own circle of young friends was also being wrenched apart, the individuals scattered by the movements of war. One Monday in July, Dhr. Spetter received an official letter: the whole household was to pack their bags and report to the Jewish Council that Wednesday. Riekie flew off to tell Anky the news in person. Since June 30th telephones had been cut off at any household in which the head of the home had the telltale "J" on his identity card.

"Only three days' notice! It doesn't seem as if it was really happening to us! They sent us a horrible little list of the clothes we are allowed to take; things like two pairs of socks and a drinking cup and food for three days—just a short list of almost nothing. My brother says it will be like a *Verkenner* camp but we don't know where they are taking us."

Anky felt herself go cold. It would be a concentration camp, one of the places of so-called protective custody that were jerry-built after the 1933 Reichstag fire. They were useful places to put Jews, Communists and a grab-bag of other suspects when civil liberties were first suspended.

"I had read books before the war about concentration camps," Anky remembered later, "but it—it seemed so impossible what happened there, so you didn't always believe it. Then when someone you know has to go there, you won't talk about it. There were reports in the papers about cruel things but I don't think people believed them."

Now the danger had to be openly acknowledged and Anky came straight to the point. "Riekie, listen, stay here with us! We have room for you, really we do! You can share the room with Addie and me and hide in that place I showed you behind the wall in the attic. You can be our *onderduikers*. Stay here, Riekie; don't go! Don't you want to be home in Den Haag when Hans comes back? Somehow I'm sure we can find a place for your parents. And your sister. And your brother . . . and your younger brother . . ." Anky's voice began to trail away. She looked helplessly round the small neat room, then back at her friend.

Riekie said, "You cannot hide us all; you know that very well. And you know something else very well: I will not leave my family. Daddy's Freemason Lodge offered to help us but it would make trouble for too many people."

"Please consider it, Riekie! For Hans' sake, so you are here when he—"

"No. We cannot live with you. We cannot all live *on* you like fleas on a dog. It would mean using your money and your food and giving you nothing but danger. How could you get forged food tickets for us all!"

"Let us at least try."

"Anky, I tell you it is impossible. We will not put you into such danger. We will not divide our family and you cannot

68

hide us all. Oh, don't worry about us; we will be going to an *Arbeitslager*, a Work Camp."

"Those are not good places. You know the rumours."

"Rumours, yes, but today everything is rumours. We will be all right. We are willing to work and we can work, so why shouldn't we all go and stay in a camp for a while when they tell us to? Maybe Hennie can lend me her gumboots." She sighed. "It will be hard for my parents to leave the house and all their things in it, but we can manage."

"Can we at least help by storing things for you?"

"No, thank you, Anky, even that would mean danger for you. My father already took the seder dishes and menorah candlestick to my cousins and they will take them to—" She broke off with a smile and a shrug. These days, even best friends found it best not to tell one another everything.

"Very well then, I will come and see you when you are packing tomorrow evening."

When Tuesday evening came, it still didn't seem real. Anky looked at her friend and family as they stepped over the growing pile of suitcases in their living room.

"They took too much luggage," she remembered, "they took far too much. Everyone did. I think that was the worst thing about the war, what they did to the Jews."

In the Amsterdam Museum of Jewish History there are photographs of families leaving for transit camps; schoolboys in caps and mufflers, young children in pushchairs, everyone with bags of extra belongings tied round their backs with string. A photo shows young Jewish people in the transit camp where Riekie went. The boys are in prayer caps, all solemn faced. They are gathered round a table where one young man is lighting the Hannukah candles. It is a scene to break your heart.

In the Spetter living room the twelve-year-old boy was trying to cram one more adventure book into his case. "You cannot wear books," said his father, "It will be a Work Camp. You will be kept busy for a change. Come and sit on my case so I can close it."

"Oh Riekie," said Anky, "if only Hans was here to say goodbye to you."

Riekie was wearing Hennie's gumboots. Her hair was dishevelled. "Will you say goodbye for me? No, it may not be necessary. Who knows, we may meet in Poland; the world is small. We'll both be back, Anky, and we'll play bridge again and listen to Jelly-Roll Morton twenty times in an evening!" Her bright little face grew serious, "Don't be concerned for me. You see, I am taking a Bible with me." She slipped it into her suitcase and closed the catch.

"Oh, a Bible—what good can that do?"

"It means so much to Hans now; he talked to me about it and sent postcards. So don't be worried about me. I have a Bible wherever I go."

Next morning she was taken to Westerbork, a transit camp in the north-east Netherlands, where pasture land had been reclaimed from primeval peat bog by the ingenious Benedictines. The irony of Westerbork is that it was built by the Dutch. In the thirties so many Jewish families were fleeing west out of Nazi Germany that they were temporarily housed in a central internment camp in Westerbork till permanent jobs and homes could be found. Now the Nazis were using the camp for transit in the other direction and some of the Jews who had fled ten years earlier were seeing Westerbork for the second time.

During the Occupation ninety-three trains left Westerbork, heading east. Each was packed with a thousand people. Sometimes families managed to keep together; sometimes they were torn apart. Eighteen months after Riekie Spetter left Westerbork, Anne Frank travelled the same journey. Of the Jews who passed through the transit camp, four thousand survived the war.

Somehow Riekie managed to scribble a note to the Rookmaakers. She slipped it out of the train as it carried her to an unknown destination. The addressed envelope was picked up by the side of the track by a Dutch patriot who put a stamp on it and posted it to Den Haag. There Theodora and Henderik read the message of hope, "Good and healthy. So far we are being quite well treated." Later, Theodora was to use that letter for a sinister purpose. As they read it, Riekie stood, wedged upright, in one of the hot shrieking cattle trucks, with a Bible in her little suitcase and warm memories of Hans in her heart.

After the war, the Dutch commissioned a memorial for all those who had passed through Westerbork on a one-way trip: a length of railway tracks that end suddenly, twisted up into the air like a pair of arms reaching for help. The events of Hans Rookmaaker's early manhood drove him to look for an explanation. If God had control over history, it would make sense out of sorrow.

Of course Riekie's friends tried to trace the family. The Red Cross was inundated with such requests throughout the war. They did what they could but their word was a regretful, "Wait. From Westerbork families are being transported all over Nazi Europe. Reports are filtering in slowly. Please wait."

That was not good enough for Theodora. She went to a local fortune-teller. What the Red Cross could not find out, she would discover by more devious means. The fortune-teller instructed her to return, bringing with her something that Riekie had owned. Now it is possible that the girl had left a scarf or pair of gloves at Hans' parent's home, but the one thing we know that was there was the letter she had written and tossed out of the freight-train.

The fortune-teller applied herself to the question, gave her answer and collected her fee. Months went by and there was still no news. Theodora returned to her local divining woman several times. The answer was always the same: "Riekie will come back."

How do these things work: a lying word from a servant of the father of lies, or something breathing from the page that echoed the girl's thoughts as she scribbled the words? Maybe it was wishful thinking from Theodora herself that tipped the scale towards a more hopeful message. Whatever the explanation, the fortune-teller's conclusion was enough to keep hope alive in Theodora's mind. Her son's special girl had been taken away; after the war the mother was still convincing herself, "Riekie will come back."

People who have never lived under an occupying power mentally divide the civilian population into two groups, the goodies and the baddies. On one hand there are the loyal Resistance fighters. On the other hand there are the nasty collaborators. According to this scenario, committed Christians help to hide Jews while atheistic traitors turn them over to fellow Nazis. The situations of real life are more complex. They are also more interesting.

During the Occupation, there were loyal Dutch with Christian convictions who did not hide Jews in their homes. There were many without clear Christian faith who did. Among them were Anky's parents. Hiding *onderduikers* was a dangerous game. By the end of the war, Anky Huiker had a story of being kept safe and alive that matched Hans' experience in the Oranje Hotel. When God prepares a man for His service, He also prepares his wife.

The breakfast things were barely cleared away when Anky's sister happened to glance out of the window. "German soldiers next door!"

The row of house-plants on the Huitkers' front window-sill screened six anxious pairs of eyes as the whole household peered down from the first floor to their neighbour's house. Sure enough, Nazi soldiers were standing in the street, the doors of their car stood open.

"Look, look, they are bringing them out!"

They watched their neighbours, betrayed and cuffed from their home and pushed into the car. "There's only Dhr. van der Hengst—is Mevr. van der Hengst not going too? There are Ronni's mother and father! Just think, if she was an *onderduiker* there instead of here—" (Ronni's parents were taken to Westerbork where they were among the 900 prisoners who were still alive there after the war.)

Anky spoke to Mevr. Wolf and her son. "They may not come here as well today. It's only a small car." The car was full. The Huitkers and their two *onderduikers* melted back from the window as the Nazis and their prey drove fast down the street.

"Come, we must live as though the day was normal." Mevr. Huitker strode towards her kitchen, "I will go and comfort Mevr. van der Hengst when the street is clear."

Her husband sank into his chair, illness weakening him

more than it should have done because of the lack of food. Their *onderduikers* had to eat but even with the help of the occasional cheese from the Wolfs' friends on a northern farm, they could only just manage. The entrance to the hiding place could not be seen when the ladder was pulled up but the sudden raid next door brought the danger so close. It could have been them. There must be a traitor in the street.

Addie said to the Jewish young man by her side, "I'll go to the Wellemans and tell them they have to hide you and your mother now."

Their eyes met. "Be careful for your sake as well as for ours."

She nodded and ran down the steep stairs to the door. Anky was flinging on her coat. "I think I have time to warn Ronni not to come back here this evening. Try to relax, Father, they may not come here after all."

A town clock struck the quarter and Anky put on a little speed, her small figure in neatly mended clothes stepping purposefully through the morning crowd. Other Den Haag citizens were making their way to work. Anky was on more serious business.

"Ronni?" Her boyfriend's mother opened the door. "No, she isn't here, Anky. Probably with Hank. What's the trouble?"

Anky told her briefly and sped off, dodging through the morning crowds. Ronni must not come home to her house after work or she could fall into a Nazi trap.

A tall blond Dutchman opened the door this time and Anky repeated her questions.

"Ronni? No, she isn't here any more." He had a friendly smile. "I know how hard it is trying to trace a friend these days. Ronni may drop in later. Step inside a minute and get your breath."

"I was afraid I'd be late for work but I wanted to see Ronni first."

"Then it must be something important. You could leave a message with me. I'm going to be here all day."

"Oh, that is kind of you. Then I won't have to phone from work. Could you tell her not to come back to the Huitkers'

73

house tonight. If she could stay here, then maybe after tomorrow we could—"

"Maybe you could find somewhere safer for her," he finished her words, "As they say, 'It's only by diving under that you can keep your head above water'."

"That's right." They shared the joke that was known to all loyal Dutch.

For the rest of the day Anky put the matter out of her mind as she tried to push aside the familiar pangs of hunger.

"It was not easy to live then," she remembered later, "but these are not the things that you remember as being hard in the war. It's just that all your friends went away."

All that day she found satisfaction in letters well-typed and memos correctly filed; as evening came she went home in peace. She skirted the strange bicycle leaning outside the front door and let herself in. At the top of the stairs stood a man she knew by sight. The tall blond Dutchman was a member of the Dutch Nazi Party.

Her mother was weeping while Addie tried to comfort her. Her father, pale and ill, had his arm gripped tightly by the hand of the treacherous Netherlander.

"Ah, so you have come home. We know you have been hiding Jews. You cannot deny it after what you told me this morning." He jerked the older man's arm and moved towards the door. "Now you Jew-lover, come with me!"

Suddenly his way was blocked by a small furious figure. "You shall not take my father away," said Anky Huitker, "He is old. He is ill. You cannot be so ridiculous! Yes, we hid Jews in our home and we will hide them again if we can, but it was not my father who hid them. The Jews were my friends. If there is guilt, let it be my guilt. You will not take my father! Take me!"

CHAPTER EIGHT

Philosophy and Fleas

HANS ROOKMAAKER'S FIRST impression of Stanislau prison was the smell. It was strong but puzzling; why should a Nazi prison smell of bitter almonds? "It's the lice," said a fellow prisoner, "Look!" Scores of typhoid lice, a quarter of an inch long, grey and disgusting, were slowly climbing up and down the inside walls.

The POWs went through the usual procedure when they arrived; they were stripped, medically examined, de-loused and had their hair cut off. Then they were photographed, holding a slate with their number scrawled on it.

The building they were put in was old enough to have been put to better use. Before the Nazis took it over, it had been a monastery. Now the rows of small windows looked out onto an exercise yard with a latrine pit big enough to sink two double-decker buses. When the wind blew from the pit towards the building, not even the scented lice could compete. Between the yard and the rest of the world rose a high wall topped with rows of barbed wire. Two metres inside it a four-metre screen of wire cut Hans' view into barbed squares. Above the wall was a wooden catwalk for the patrolling guards and a tower at each corner with a searchlight. On each tower a machine gun crouched under a tarpaulin cover. It was not unlike Nuremberg, except that it looked more permanent.

Hans, the studious, elegantly-born Haagener, went about the compound like the others, a thin blanket pulled round his shoulders. Occasionally he took it off and shook it vigorously, but it was no use. As soon as he put it on or huddled under it at night, he was attacked by an army of fleas.

The days at Stanislau took on their own pattern. The first waking half hour was spent hammering at fleas and lice. Then, with the circulation well roused, the men stood in rows of five for roll call. The food came twice a day and it was better than at Nuremberg, though a diet of 1500 calories a day was not enough. There was a meagre but steady supply of cigarettes from Red Cross parcels. Hennie was of the post-war opinion that her brother had more cigarettes in the POW camp than she did in Den Haag.

"Rookmaaker?" said one of the prisoners one day, "There's another man here with that name. Wonder if you two know each other?" The other Rookmaaker was Hans' cousin Dan. Now, instead of being a faceless unit without origin, Hans had someone to talk to. They tramped around the compound together in the thin winter sun, reliving shared jokes of family birthdays and Sinterklaas days. Dan was only a distant cousin but his brother knew Dora. Hans' faceless feeling began to lift a little; the life he had lived in Den Haag became less dreamlike as he and Dan shared memories.

Dan dug his hands into his pockets and stared at the wire, "There's going to be a tunnel. I'm going to get out."

"Where?"

"If you're not in on it, I daren't tell you, for your own safety. Sorry, Hans, but it's better that way."

Hans understood, but he was conscious of a selfish reluctance growing inside him. He didn't want Dan to escape and leave him inside the wire.

Somehow the men managed to celebrate Sinterklaas Day. Cigarettes were carefully wrapped and placed in a friend's shoe beside his bunk. Some of the married men wept into their blankets as they thought of their children on this day.

Christmas came and it brought music to the little world inside the wire. Even though a pagan festival had replaced the Birth of Christ on official Nazi calendars, German memories ran deeper. "Silent night, holy night; all is calm, all is bright." Prisoners and guards joined in as humanity and memory of shared faith drew them together.

As the Dutchmen sang one of their traditional carols,

Hans thought of the previous Christmas with his friends in Den Haag.

> O Sion's daughter, where art thou?
> Good news have I to tell thee,
> A greater joy I bring thee now,
> Than ever yet befell thee.

Then New Year dawned: 1944. As always, the pessimists looked back, the optimists forward. When the days lengthened, there was mysterious activity among the prisoners. A set of clothes and rags was sewn into a life-sized doll. With a wool hat pulled down and a muffler pulled up, it would be indistinguishable from the other ragged men in the edgy light of morning and evening roll call.

Hans bade an unobtrusive goodbye to Dan, giving him messages for family and friends. He flinched from the thought of facing prison life without his cousin, but nursed a hopeless hope that Dan would meet friendly Poles or Russians outside the wire.

"Wish me luck."

"Good luck, Dan." Their social behaviour pattern, learned from childhood, made them want to shake hands but it was too formal a sign of parting. They turned away from each other in the compound and did not look back.

Next day the doll was wedged between the chest of one prisoner and the back of another, to take its place in roll call. The guard paced down the lines of men, counting, "*Fünf . . . zehn . . . fünfzehn . . . zwanzig . . .*" The guard paced on to the next block of prisoners and the next, ". . . *vierzig . . . fünf 'n vierzig . . . fünfzig . . .*" It had worked. The doll, with other tricks and diversions, fooled the guards for two days. During that time, six men escaped.

On the third day the prisoners were suddenly ordered out of the building. They stood bareheaded in the biting wind while the guards screamed at them, "Men have got out! You thought to make fools of us—us the Master-race!" One guard cracked out an order and the covers were ripped from the machine guns. The grey gleaming shapes crouched like panthers above the men on the ground.

A prisoner stepped out of line and the guns immediately swung round to point at him. He spoke loudly and in good German, "You dare not shoot us in cold blood. If you do, a report will be made known to the Geneva Convention. Even in war, there are rules of humanity." The first man to frame laws of war was the Dutchman, Hugo Grotius, who based them on the rational nature common to all mankind.

For a moment the stalemate at Stanislau held the actors in a tableau of imminent death. Then the guns were covered again and the order to dismiss let the prisoners go back inside the building. Hans looked at the familiar faces, missing the member of his family more than ever. If only Dan could get away fast enough.

The prisoners who escaped were betrayed and caught. Dan was shot.

Finally even Hans' own solitude was too much for him. Deep within the Noordzee mussel of the man, some reserve broke down and he wrote a long letter to Dora. For page after page he poured out his sorrow for Dan, his hopes and fears for life, the first steps of his faith in Christ, his love for Riekie and his concern for her.

Millions of letters crossed wartime Europe under the compassionate auspices of the Red Cross. They took from three months to a year to arrive. Hans' long outpouring to Dora was one of the letters that never reached its destination. After the war, Dora tried to find out something of her brother's experiences and thoughts behind the wire. The answer was invariably, "But I told you already in that letter I sent."

"And *I* told *you* it never arrived. So now you must say it to me."

"No. I already wrote it." The *dijk* had been breached once. It would not be allowed to spill over again.

Winter eased into spring in the Polish Ukraine and the compound grew muddy as the ground thawed. The men played volleyball and football, the Germans obligingly kicking the ball back when it strayed beyond the wire. As the Polish sun grew warmer the fleas grew more joyously active. The men carried their bedding outside, shook it and draped it over the wire. The periodic puffings of DDT by the Nazis was no more than a rearguard action.

Meanwhile the armies of the Third Reich were, in their own words, "shortening the front line". The prisoners, crouched over their hidden radios, put another meaning on the words, "They're being beaten back! The Russians are moving in!"

There were seven radios hidden about Stanislau prison and the wall of one room was covered with a handdrawn chart of Europe with lines of troop movements that were redrawn every time there was news. The prisoners delighted to compare what they heard from German radio with what they managed to pick up from the BBC.

A prisoner's hand, rough and ingrained with dirt, delicately adjusted the handmade knob on the handmade dial. "Almost . . . there, got it. Ssh!" The chimes of Big Ben were unmistakable. Queen Wilhelmina would be hearing them too, thought the men. Then the clear Home Counties tones of the announcer came through, "This . . . is the nine o'clock news and this is Alvar Liddell reading it."

Reception varied but the gist of the news was clear. The Russians were in Poland, reoccupying the land the Nazis had taken in 1942. The Nazis were retreating from the Eastern Front. As summer became the autumn of 1944 the changes of war penetrated the prisoners' own lives. With scant warning they were told to pack and leave the camp.

Hans struggled into his outdoor clothes. Better to wear them all than risk losing a bundle en route. He stood in the compound with the others, looking at the tops of the familiar pinetrees. Where next? The order was given and they were marched towards the railway station. A Nazi soldier tramped wearily beside the column of ragged men. "I'd rather transport a bag of fleas than a consignment of Dutch POWs."

At the station they were packed into goods-trains, stumbling forward into the darkness, kicking up dust from the straw on the floor. Hans could just make out the shape of a little wood-burning stove like the one in the Nuremberg hut. A large lidless can stood in one corner, doubtless for a toilet. Hans hoped fervently that the journey would not be long. Next moment the doors were clanged shut.

The journey was long. The train rumbled on for hours and days. From time to time the doors were opened, letting in blessed air and light. The can was passed through the crowd of men, sloshed out beside the track, and passed back in. Food, of sorts, was provided and the men fumbled it from one another's hands in their deep twilight, jolting world.

They huddled in the straw, making fruitless guesses at their destination. France? Italy? The only real things in their limbo were the rumbling of the goods-train, the stench of the can and the pricking of the familiar fleas. Hans carried with him the reality of God.

The train stopped and the doors were flung open. "Out! *Raus! Raus!*"

They fell out, stiff and dazed, the noise of the train still bumbling in their ears. "Where are we?" One of the guards shoved them into a manageable column and gave the order to march. They stumbled over railway sidings and through a goods-yard. Someone spotted a station signpost and everyone adjusted himself in relationship to the map of Europe. They were in Neu Brandenburg, up near the Baltic coast. Several men turned their heads longingly towards the west. The Netherlands lay only two hundred and fifty kilometres away.

Hans settled into yet another POW camp. Before Stanislau and Nuremberg and Breda he would remember a life that included home cooking, jazz records and dancing, with Riekie's blonde head close to his cheek. It was like remembering a childhood fairy tale.

As soon as he began to explore the camp compound he knew he had something to look forward to. There was a library. It was only a pile of assorted books in one of the huts, but there was a library commission chosen from among the men to order selected books through the Red Cross. Hans made himself known to the librarian. "What have you got that will help me with Naval Officer studies? I want to finish the course I began at Den Helder."

The librarian showed him and recommended some

prisoners he should contact. The list of names included people who had been instructors in more peaceful times. Hans set out in search of his new teachers. Before long a course of studies had been mapped out and he set to work. Some of the prisoners fussed over homemade saws and wirecutters, hankering after freedom, while others began their games of Monopoly and bridge. Hans was among the studious ones, filling the days with study, debate and reflection. His sponge-like brain revelled in the uninterrupted hours of mental effort.

With the Naval studies completed, he sat his exam, invigilated by one of the prisoners. His papers were sent to the Netherlands through the Red Cross where they were marked and returned. Hans passed well, as usual.

Sometime during this period Hans' life took a turn towards his eventual life-work. One of the prisoners, Captain (later Professor) Mekkes laid four solid volumes before the young man. Hans read the titles, *"A New Critique of Theoretical Thought* by Herman Dooyeweerd."

Mekkes briefly laid out Dooyeweerd's philosophic position. "He thinks as a Christian, not as a rationalist. I know you have been reading Kant. Now try Dooyeweerd."

Later he came across Hans again and asked, "Well, how is your study?"

The young man summed up what he had read so far, his brown eyes gleaming with suppressed excitement. Mekkes did not push him. "Yes, this is a good thinker to mould your mind. Let me suggest a couple of lines of approach for you. Then study on your own and come and see me when you are ready to talk further."

Hans returned to the four volumes like a man long-starved who cannot bear to leave the table till every crumb is eaten. His faith in Christ, once relatively unsophisticated, acquired a firm underpinning of philosophic thought. In Scheveningen he had found a place to stand. In Dooyeweerd, he found a structure of thought that could encompass his whole world. Twenty-eight years later, in an interview, Hans Rookmaaker acknowledged his debt to the philosopher:

81

"I'm a pupil of Dooyeweerd. What he has discovered has given me a better answer to many things than most other philosophies because it is more open; it's not such a narrow description of reality. Most philosophers try to approach everything from history or from physics or from morality. But in his philosophy all things come better into their place.

"When I became a Christian just by reading the Bible, there was nobody around to help me. At the same time as reading the Bible I was studying philosophy. So I came to the point where I said: Well, the Bible gives me all the answers I need, but Kant is very interesting. If I become a Christian, can I also be a Kantian?

"Then somebody pointed out, 'Why don't you read Dooyeweerd?' His first twenty pages utterly convinced me that Christianity was right, because they showed me that Kant was a religion in himself, in that he took a point of view. He was not just a neutral thinker based on a neutral logic; he started from a point of view just as Christianity does. Knowing this liberates you to make a choice of points of view. I'm very thankful to Dooyeweerd for this."

Hans acquired a notebook from the Red Cross supplies and began to fill it with notes and Old Testament references. His love of the prophets began at this time. He filled the notebook and began on another, debating every point with Mekkes and feeling his mind grow as he had time to follow every idea and issue to its limit. A Nazi POW camp might not have seemed the ideal place to study Christian philosophy but Hans Rookmaaker made it so.

A generation later he wrote to a composer, warning against the trap of idleness till the imagined perfect moment for scholarship or for creation:

"Don't be afraid. Make it as good as you can . . . you can't do better . . . and it will be a step to the next one, etc. Only in working and trying our work grows. And also our ideas and insights. We cannot wait for the perfect aesthetics and frame of mind and then start . . . it probably will never even get in that direction if we don't start now. The only point that matters is the *Way* . . . the way we go. With the Lord. In confidence."

1944 turned into 1945 and the armies of the thousand-year Reich were shrinking back towards their own country. Chased over the border from the Netherlands, the Nazis scorched the face of the earth in their wake, stripping the land of cars, bicycles and railway lines, and destroying every bridge when they had crossed it.

"Not a German stalk of wheat is to feed the enemy," Hitler had declared the previous autumn. "He is to find every footbridge destroyed, every road blocked—nothing but death, annihilation and hatred will meet him." The Nazis retreated like Satan from Calvary, destroying every foot of the way.

In the west of the Netherlands, the population is heaviest and the duneland cannot grow food crops. People collapsed from hunger in the streets of Amsterdam, Rotterdam and Den Haag. One Dutch woman I spoke to remembers how her mother dug worms from the garden to chop and fry with a little rice. "They tasted bristly."

In January 1945 Henderik Rookmaaker died of a heart attack, tense and weary with the war. People's supplies of food were gone and money could not buy what did not exist. Theodora and the Huitker family were levelled to a similar standard of life: one cup of soup a day if you queued for it in the street like a dosser.

The Huitker family with their *onderduikers* tuned their radio hidden in the dressmaker's dummy. Their Queen, safe in Britain, spoke to them: "The Netherlands will rise again." Underground transmitters in their own country broadcast, "Here is Radio Oranje, the voice of the fighting Netherlands." The Huitkers glanced nervously towards the wall separating their house and the house next door. You could not be sure of your neighbours these days. They took it in turns to get the daily cups of soup, walking slowly from weakness. The prisoners at Neu Brandenburg heard the news from the Netherlands on their radios and shuddered. Thanks to the Red Cross they were eating better than the people at home.

Rookmaaker and the grey-haired Mekkes strolled the compound weaving philosophical ideas with the revelation of God. What with individual tuition and lack of competing interests, Hans was being given an education he could not have received anywhere else. Week in, week out, there was nothing to do but attend roll call, eat two quick meals a day and study. He was nostalgic for that pattern of day for the rest of his life. Guns boomed in the background of his mind, but Dooyeweerd and Isaiah spoke louder.

"Come on, get out of here!" Some prisoners were shouting at him. "The Russians are going to liberate the camp and the Nazis are fighting back!"

Hans emerged from his books and tuned his mind to the present. There was a steady bump-thump of guns. The men hustled him outside where they met another group running from the radio hut. "We heard the broadcast! Stay where we are, they said, or we'll get caught in the crossfire!"

A shell whistled over their heads. They threw themselves flat and wriggled for cover. Windows in one hut were shattered as a shell answered from the other direction. "Quick, the ditch by the earthwall over by the wire!"

They made a break for it and rolled in, pressing themselves to the ground beside the rest of the men. There was some cursing and shoving as they made room for each other, then there was nothing to do but wait. The sounds of war came closer. Trees were splintered as a tank edged towards the wire. Hans pressed his face to the bottom of the ditch, smelling the springtime in the earth while war screamed above his head in the blue sky of April.

The Nazis, like a grey wolf at bay, spat and snarled their guns in the face of Russian strength. The prisoners wondered if the whole camp would be massacred rather than be released. Would this ditch be their grave? Such things had happened.

There was a lull in the firing and they heard a Slavic accented voice through a loudhailer, "Give up or we shoot the place flat." The reply came from inside the compound as the German Commandant stated his terms. "No. I stay."

The Russians set up batteries all round the camp and moved in foot by foot and yard by yard. Incendiary shells shattered the roof of the library hut and flames licked through the windows like the tongue of a hungry cat. The glow of fire lit up the April dusk with dancing shadows across the compound. Darkness fell as the war rolled over Hans' head. How fortunate that his precious notebooks were on his bunk. It would be a shame to lose all those notes.

Was it imagination or were the sounds less than before? After a while the men were sure the tide had turned. The Commandant spoke through the loudhailer, "I surrender." Then the next half hour was confusion and joy.

Russian infantry men in padded clothes and balaklava hats tore down the hated wire and burst into the compound. Hans and the other man leapt from their ditch like resurrected souls. With arms round each other, liberators and liberated danced and hugged each other in the firelight. Human communication was reduced to the waving of hands, the exchange of cigarettes and the strong wild laughter of men set free.

The Russians were pitifully equipped; they strolled around the compound, their rifles tucked under their arms and ammunition loose in their pockets. With padded clothes and bearded faces they looked more like hunters than soldiers as they inspected the nearby town of Neu Brandenburg in the light of dawn. It was April 28th 1945. For Hans Rookmaaker, the war was over.

The next few days went by in a whirl of work as the ex-prisoners helped to set Neu Brandenburg on its feet again. The town had been badly damaged by both armies. Hans and the other men worked with Soviet soldiers rebuilding the bakery, laying water pipes and setting up a temporary electricity supply. Hans' engineering training was put to good use. During May groups of men said goodbye as lorries were arranged to take them home. Finally it was Hans' turn to leave. With fourteen other men he sat on a narrow bench along the inside of an army lorry. The Russian driver, singing bawdy songs (at least that is what they sounded like) drove day and night to unload his charges at the frontier. There they were medically inspected and puffed for fleas, the nozzle of the DDT gun forcing a cloud of white powder up each sleeve, each trouser leg and down the neck. The powder stayed on the skin for hours and the vermin were as defeated as the Master-race.

Nearer home, English troops took over from the Russians, "Here we are, then. Sorry I can't speak your lingo, old chaps, but you can understand me, so that's all right. Now, all aboard for the Skylark. Thirteen, fourteen—there, that's the lot. Righty-ho, driver. Happy landings!"

The number of men dwindled as they were dropped off near their home towns. Then the call came from the front of the lorry, "Next stop, The Hague. OK, mate?"

"OK, er, mate," said the ragged young man in the back. Hans Rookmaaker was almost home. The view from the windows of the lorry soothed his spirit like a familiar song. Already the prisoner's world of mud and wire seemed far away.

Later that day Hans soaked in a hot bath. It was not the familiar bathroom at Ranonkelstraat. The Nazi's tank road had forced the Rookmaakers to move to a red brick house in Prinz Hendrieksplein, but it was home nevertheless. The blue and white Chinese vases in the living room, the Indonesian carvings and brasses were intact, giving Hans continuity that linked back to the childhood days of sunlight on white marble.

He missed his father. His mother's widowhood was only three months old; she was muddled with sorrow and kept babbling something about a fortune-teller. Hans counted his ribs and looked ruefully at the festering fleabites that dotted his skin from head to foot. Back in his room he dressed in clean clothes, which hung on him like sacks. The young man of twenty-three weighed less than the young fellow of twenty-one. Decent shoes were still painful but he bore the discomfort; it was time to get back to normal society. He stepped outside the house to visit friends.

Like other ex-POWs, Hans expected to be returning home to the Holland he had left in 1942. That Holland was not there any more. The changes he had seen at the beginning of the Occupation were more marked after five years of Nazi law. With no cars there was a Sabbath hush to the wide streets. Houses were unpainted and some shop-fronts were boarded up. There were traces of a roughly painted sign on a house wall, "The Jew Levi lived here." A man pedalled by on a bicycle; the pedals creaked rhythmically and the wheels were tyred with old rope wrapped about the rims. Trees had been cut down for fuel, making the polite squares of Den Haag look suspicious and bare. Food had been so scarce there were no cats or dogs to sun themselves on domestic doorsteps. The proportion of women to men was high as husbands and sons had disappeared by conscription or the razzia. Everyone had lost someone.

Hans found his country had changed and so had he. Dora put the change into words. "I think he had learned to listen. There's one thing that Hans could do very well as he grew older and that's listen."

Anky Huitker moved round her parents' living room, handing out coffee. The cups were not full and the brew was not strong but it was real coffee, dropped from the sky in the food parcels the Allies had flown in. It was a treat that friends were free to visit friends again. She looked a second time at the young man sitting silently in a corner.

"Is it? Yes, it is Hans! You have come home safe!" They shook hands. "How was it in Poland and Germany? We got a little news from your mother."

"It was cold."

"No good, Anky," a mutual friend laughed, "He won't talk much. It's the same old Hans."

Anky sat beside him and spoke quietly, "You know they took Riekie away?"

"Mother said something."

"After Westerbork they went to some place in Poland. That was all the Red Cross could find out. Riekie thought it would be an Arbeitslager."

"Was it?"

"I—we don't know, Hans. That's what is so terrible. We heard rumours about the place but I don't know if I can believe them."

"What was the name?"

"Auschwitz."

In 1945 the name meant little to them. Soviet troops had liberated the death camp that January and their report was published in May. But even when the facts were known, the horror of Hitler's Final Solution and the magnitude of the numbers that were gassed, anaesthetised belief. In a way, it still does.

A generation later in her Den Haag apartment, Dora closed one photo album and opened another. "Hans is a person who doesn't know someone so very quickly. It takes a long, long time. And it takes people a long time to know him because he never will talk about himself. He and Anky, they were happy together in a special way, but I think he had a rough time to forget Riekie." Her eyes rested for a moment on a framed picture of her brother that stood on a side table. "No, he never did forget Riekie. I think he was missing her all his life."

CHAPTER NINE

The Right Wife

"No, I don't remember when he proposed," said Anky, "I don't think he even proposed at all. At a certain time we thought it better to be engaged. It went very gradually. We were nothing much to each other when the war was immediately over. It was just that he was one of the ones who came back and that was very special, of course, because most of the friends did not come back."

The years after Liberation had a limbo quality for many people in the Netherlands. It was not the peace of pre-war. Many had to live with silence, not knowing if they were free to marry or remarry, mourn, hope or despair or wait. Hennie's precious hoard of unroasted coffee beans had long since been scooped from the bottom of the Chinese vase. Food from the Allies' air-lift had to be eked out till agriculture and imports could get back to normal. Rations included such dubious delicacies as whalemeat and tinned snoek.

Hans, trying to settle down, found he had changed inside himself with the enforced maturity of a youth that has lived through war. One writer has said, "Nearly every ex-POW will claim that he learned more of human nature in a couple of years than in two decades of normal life."

As the Netherlands staggered back to normal life, Hans and his friends found things to do. When the first American film was shown in Den Haag, he went to it with Anky Huitker. It seemed that wherever Hans went, the neat, dark-haired secretary went too. People began to take their coupleness for granted even before they did. They spent a lot of time talking. Hans had convictions about life that intrigued Anky but also made her furious.

"I don't believe it! The Bible does not say Jesus is the only way to God! Why, I never heard of the idea before!"

Hans showed her verse after verse. She argued, he explained. They shifted to her idea that Christ was one of several incarnations, like Siva, Lord of the Dance. Hans explained that Jesus is unique. "You see, the Bible does teach these things. I am right and you are wrong."

Anky was loathe to admit it. She lost sleep over those arguments.

"It was not easy for me to say that I am wrong," she said later, "but that was the beginning of our real friendship, because that gives you such a bond, of course, when you believe the same. Otherwise I don't think I would ever have married him. We had big arguments because I didn't want it to be true as he said. But you must see for yourself; it is in the Bible that Jesus is the only way that you come to God."

One of the first times Anky went to church was when she went with Hans to see him baptised and confirmed. "When first you believe these things you want to tell other people and especially your own family whom you love most. Then you overdo it, knowing too little but trying too hard. We both overdid it; I with my family and Hans with his."

After a while it became a dangerous liability to invite Hans (and therefore Anky too) to any friendly gathering. Before long the conversation had worked its way round to religion. Hans' enthusiasm knew no bounds. The Dutch can become highly inflamed over tiny details of philosophy, politics or religion, but remain good friends at the end of the evening. Arguing politics and religion is a national sport comparable to British pub arguments about the relative merits of football teams or breweries. It is said that if two Dutchmen are in a room they will form a debating society; if there are three they will form a political party or a new denomination.

One evening Hennie, her husband and a friend cornered Hans and almost brought him to a standstill. "The trouble with all you severe Calvinists," his sister told him, "is that you don't have anything to believe; it is all stuff that you say you *know*. You and your propaganda!"

"Look," said the friend, "it's like this; let us say we are together in a room and before us there is a trunk. It is closed. You say you know there is a chicken in the trunk. But I say maybe it is a rabbit. That is the difference between us: you know but I *believe*."

Hans retreated to Calvinist philosophy, beginning with the known point: God, and working from there to verbal revelation.

"We Liberal Protestants believe the Bible too," reminded his brother-in-law, "but just not every word as you do." They threw difficulties in his path and Hans began to re-think his tight position. Maybe Jonah was not a figure of history—but how to determine from the text itself which way to read the words? We bring our subjective minds to it and those minds are formed by our own place in history.

"I'll have to think a bit more," he admitted.

Hennie looked at him kindly, "So the answer is for you to study even more? Well, hard work is in the family; you know I always work like a fool too. But, Hansje, you don't talk of anything else but religion. You have lost your gaiety since Poland. Mummy wants to know what you are going to do with your life. Are you going to be a preacher?"

It was now a year after the war and Hans Rookmaaker was a young man of twenty-four. Theodora tackled him on the subject of his future. "What's wrong with the Marines, dear? After all, you had all that good training in Den Helder. It does seem a pity to waste it. Whatever am I going to say to my friends when they ask me what my twenty-four-year-old son does for a living? Are you going to start training for something new?"

The answer was yes. Hans had been looking at the Reformed Christian world. He had noticed that there were many school teachers and that missionary activity was quite ordinary; there were theological professors and writers and preachers. His mind hovered tentatively over music history but rejected the idea when he found he would have to master a musical instrument first.

Art history? The subject had first attracted him in Neu Brandenburg. Now he was home he had time to think about

91

it in relationship to his career. There didn't appear to be any other Reformed people specialising in the field. It was even the other direction: Reformed people were highly suspicious of the world of the arts. That would make working in it a rare challenge.

Suppose he was to take Dooyeweerd's Christian vision and apply it to the work of artists, asking how an artist's belief in eternal truths affected his work? And was it possible to trace the history of philosophy through the work of painters and sculptors? As far as he could see, no Christian thinker had ever tried.

Hans Rookmaaker's mind chewed at the idea for months like a dog gnawing relentlessly at a bone. Then he decided on his life-work: he would be a Reformed Christian professor of art history. The subject that was to be the joy of his life for the next thirty years was chosen for an egoistic reason: he wanted to shine where no other man of his beliefs had struck a match. Hans and his mother moved to a flat in Amsterdam and he began his studies in art history.

Meanwhile Addie Huitker had married Dhr. Wolf, the Jewish young man who had survived the war as one of the *onderduikers* in Anky's parents' home. Mevr. and Dhr. Huitker decided to move to Amsterdam to be near Addie and her husband and it seemed quite natural for Anky to get in touch with Hans again.

Soon it was the mixture as before: the dark-haired secretary and the courtly young man seen everywhere together, usually arguing about religion. Again and again he gave her his view of the Atonement; that Christ died as the unique substitute for the death that mankind deserved. Anky slowly moved from doubt to belief. To be a substitute was not such a strange idea for her; on a dark wartime evening she had once put her life on the line to let someone else go free.

"You will not take my father," she had said to the Dutch Nazi, "The Jews we hid were my friends, so the guilt is mine! Leave my father alone! Take me!"

"Anky—no!" her mother screamed. All Holland knew what happened to pretty girls in Nazi prisons.

Anky planted her feet firmly in the doorway, "I will take the guilt."

"Come then!" the Nazi pushed the father aside and his fingers closed on the daughter's arm. He thrust her ahead of him down the stairs to the street. "Sit on the back of my bike."

Anky perched on the luggage carrier, holding her feet clear of the back spokes and turned her head to look back at the lighted upstairs windows of her home. Her future was not to be thought of, but she had done what was right.

The Dutch Nazi delivered her to a large room in the Police Station. Several people were pushed in after her. They ran to the stove in the middle of the room, to burn incriminating papers before they were thoroughly searched. Some hostages were Jews, turned out of their homes on a flimsy pretext. Others were Dutch patriots who had been caught trading on the black market or distributing Underground posters.

"What will happen to us, do you think?" asked Anky.

They averted their eyes and gave ominous shrugs. It was as Anky had heard. The Police Station was the first port of call that would lead the hostages to death, sudden or slow. The door opened again and again as groups of prisoners were pushed into the room. It became crowded. They edged towards the walls, stepping over one another's legs to find a place to sleep. Anky recalled the sixteenth-century ballad by Jan Campart who, in his own day, had helped Jews escape from danger:

> My cell is only two yards long
> And barely six feet wide;
> But smaller still will be the place
> Where soon I shall abide;
> Nameless I shall be resting there
> Together with my friends;
> Of eighteen, none of us will be
> Alive when daylight ends.

Anky was in the Police Station for ten days. Food was provided for them all (mostly bread and water) and there was a proper toilet. At night the hostages slept under their overcoats, huddled on the bare floor. Christian faith would have helped Anky with her fear but, like Hans in the Oranje Hotel, she didn't have any then.

The door opened. "Out!" shouted one of the Nazis. "Those six in that corner! *Raus!* Out!" The same scene was repeated throughout the day. Each time the room became less full, the voices of the prisoners taking on an echo from the bare walls and floor.

One of the prisoners leaned closer and murmured to Anky, "We know who you are, and the Underground organisation can get you out. It will take a little time but we can do it."

Anky was not an Underground worker but she was known as a helper. She hesitated. Workers were worth their weight in gold. Months of training and a developed instinct for danger made them invaluable in the network of spies, saboteurs and *onderduiker* hosts throughout the Netherlands. It was quite possible that six men or women could be caught and killed trying to rescue her.

"When they take you to prison," said the man, "it isn't possible to get you out, but from here we can do it."

She shook her head. "No. You must not risk several workers just for me." It was the last time she would be asked. He would not mount a rescue operation against the subject's will. The prisoners were taken away till Anky was left alone in a room filled with fears.

The door opened and the Dutch Nazi stepped inside, "Come with me."

Anky scrambled to her feet. "Where?"

"Home. Look, the outside door is open for you. Go home."

She was afraid of the rumours she had heard. Prisoners were shot in the back so that it looked as if they had been trying to escape. If she turned her back on the Police Station and walked into the dark street, how many steps would she be allowed to take?

"But you arrested me for hiding Jews. Now you are letting me go?"

"Don't worry; we will not arrest you again."

In a daze she walked through the door into the free night. She turned back once more. The Dutchman stood in the entrance hall; the bare bulb that hung from the ceiling lit up the swastika armband on his jacket. He had given himself to two masters. She suddenly realised he would have to live with his conscience whichever decision he made.

"Why are you letting me go?"

He shuffled his feet, looking stupid. "Oh because— because you have a nice mother."

"A nice mother! What are you talking about? How do you know I have a nice mother? You never saw her before the day you arrested me!"

"Just that you have a nice mother. I—I don't know why . . . please go, Miss Huitker. Just go away, go home." He closed the door between them.

In 1947 it was casually decided that Hans and Anky should become engaged. "We went out together," said Anky as she remembered the time, "then at a certain moment you know that you belong to each other. We were engaged for two years. It was a difficult time because we saw each other nearly every day but you always had to say goodbye in the evening."

When the announcement was first made, it was not greeted with shouts of joy. "But Anky, he's several years younger than you." "And he hasn't got a job." "And he's so stubborn." "And so religious."

Anky cut short the family comments, "And we are going to get married."

"But, Hans dear, she is older than you," said Theodora. "Besides the fortune-teller said—"

But Hans brushed divination aside and repeated what he had said. They were engaged.

"Oh well, I suppose you both know your own minds. I'm sure she's a very nice girl and all that; she came to see me when you were away. But the family is a little different from ours. I mean, one doesn't really *know* them. One never *sees* Juffrouw Huitker anywhere." But Hans had decided on his life-mate and nothing would deflect him from his purpose.

In 1948 they were still engaged and Anky was saving every guilder for their future home. As well as her daytime work, she had a part-time evening job typing for the conference of the International Council of Christian Churches. "There are people there from all over the world," she told her fiancé, "Americans, Canadians—"

He brightened up. "Americans? I wonder if there is someone I could talk to about Negro music?"

"I don't know. They seem mostly to be pastors and missionaries. I doubt if they would be interested in jazz. Still, I suppose you could try."

Next day Anky slipped into her place behind the typewriter and looked over the evening's work. She kept one eye on the people who wandered in and out of the office on business. The Conference secretary, a man in his thirties, dodged through the door to consult a time-table on the wall. Anky pounced.

"Reverend Schaeffer?"

"Yes?"

"I would like you to meet my fiancé."

The American smiled and held out his hand. "Hi. I'm Francis Schaeffer."

"Hans Rookmaaker. I wonder, do you have a little time? I wanted to meet an American who could talk to me about Negro music."

"Oh, you're interested in that? Well yes, I heard quite a lot of it when I was in school in Virginia."

"Anky," said Hans, "I'll be back in ten minutes."

Anky returned to her desk as the two men went out talking. She had initiated a friendship that was to last for the rest of Hans' life. The men did not return after ten minutes.

Next day her betrothed was beaming like a man who has discovered an oil well in his garden. "I like him very much, Anky. We were able to discuss so many things. He is a thinking Christian man. I introduced him to ideas in art and he seemed to understand at once."

"You must have talked a long time then."

He missed the gentle irony. "Yes, a very long time." The men had walked round the Amsterdam streets till well after midnight. When the conference ended the Revd. and Mrs. Schaeffer exchanged addresses with Hans and Anky, promising to keep in touch.

Hans and Anky were married on June 1st 1949, she wearing a plain grey suit that had been bought with saved-up clothing coupons. The civil wedding was at the Town Hall in the morning, the church wedding in the afternoon at the Reformed church where Hans had been baptised and where they were both members. Dora remembered that the wedding sermon was full of allusions to hell-fire. Anky regretted that the wedding sermon was not clear enough for the uncommitted members of the family attending the church service that day.

The Rookmaakers spent their honeymoon in France, staying part of the time with friends and passing their days looking at cathedral architecture in Paris, Dijon and Versailles. Architecture was part of art history and Hans felt if they had to spend precious money travelling to France, they had better see some. It was an unromantic arrangement, almost a working honeymoon, but it suited them both.

Their first home was in the attic of the Huitkers' house. Anky supported them both by continuing her job as secretary. Hans remained plunged deep in art history studies at the University of Amsterdam. His address had changed since the wedding day, and instead of a mother to cook his evening meal, he had a wife. They were photographed early in their marriage; a studious young couple, she poised over her typewriter, he poised over her shoulders.

One day Anky learnt her first hard lesson in living with Hans. She wrote a precise list of groceries for the next few days and gave it to him with the housekeeping purse. "There is the month's money, but the food will only take a very little of it." He promised not to forget to go shopping in the lunch hour.

That evening Anky came home from work, climbed the stairs to the attic room, tied on her apron, and looked round the improvised kitchen. "Well, where is the food?"

Their little home was filled with the sound of a jazz clarinet. "Food?" said Hans confusedly. He was lovingly taking a new record from its paper sleeve. A couple of splendid new art books lay on the table beneath the homemade lampshade.

"Oh, Hans, you didn't!"

"Well, they were such good bargains, a special sale. And look at this, Anky; just what I need to complete an idea I have about Gauguin!"

"Where is the rest of the money?"

"The . . . er, rest of it?"

"Yes, Hans, the rest of the housekeeping money for this whole month!"

He plunged his hands deep into pocket after pocket, looking more and more like a small boy who finds he has left his report card on the bus. "Well, there must be something left . . . oh, dear."

"You are crazy! We cannot eat books and records!" He was enough to give anyone a migraine.

"Well, there must be something in the cupboard," said the Son of the Resident, "See what you can find while I play the other side of this Woody Herman. He has a style that I never—"

"Hans, you are impossible!"

Somehow they lived out the rest of the month on Anky's ingenuity and Anky's savings. She learned never to trust him again with the housekeeping purse.

But Hans did what he did knowingly. Later, he was strolling the Amsterdam streets with a young artist friend whose father's books had been as much help to him as those of Dooyeweerd. He paused and peered into the window of a curio shop. "H'm, that is Indonesian, that little carving. It is beautiful."

They stood admiring it for a while, Anton Jaanse said, "It is expensive surely."

"Oh yes, but you must sometimes buy such things to make you be more fully human. Maybe I have spent a little too much at times on such things, and people say it is not practical. But it is more fully practical because it takes into account all reality. Sometimes you must eat a little less in order to buy a picture or a record. It would impoverish your life and at last your spiritual walk if you think only of those things that you can eat or wear.

"You would become a pauper if you did *not* buy beautiful things. Sometimes they are more important than anything else."

Anton never forgot his father's friend. "Once I needed to go to Florence to study art. Rookmaaker paid for my ticket."

CHAPTER TEN

Battle-lines

"Oh. Well. That is very nice," said Hans in December 1949.

"Very nice? Is that all you have to say? It is not every day your wife tells you such news!"

"Of course, Anky, of course. I am delighted. It is—what can I say?—it is all very wonderful."

She understood that he meant it from the heart. "But what will you do now?"

He looked blankly at her and began feeling in his pockets for his tobacco pouch. "Do? Must I do anything? You are well, are you not? You can continue with things as usual?"

"Yes, I can shop for you and cook for you and keep the place clean. But, Hans, I cannot go out to work all day with a baby to care for, unless"—her eyes danced at the impossible thought—"unless you would like to stay at home and care for it while you study?"

He practically shuddered, "Oh no, no."

"Then you must get a job that can support your family."

"Oh." Yes, he supposed he would have to. He thought wistfully of his books. He had found such a wide world to roam in, a world almost untouched by Reformed Christian thought. It seemed as though Protestants were still living in the days of the iconoclasts; unwilling, and eventually unable, to look at beauty for its own sake.

In 1947 he had hurled himself, full-tilt, at the art department's required two-year course of Latin and Greek, completing it in one year. With that done he had gone on to devour every fact and opinion of art history that had come his way, evaluating them and digesting them into an intricate filing system that stood stacked in the corners of their attic home.

So while he continued to study for his Ph.D. he got a job teaching history and art history at Leiden High School, where his own High School studies had been finished before the war. Five mornings a week he left the flat and cycled half an hour to Amsterdam Station, parked the bicycle and took a train to Leiden. There he picked up his second bicycle from the station park and cycled to the High School. The arrangement was cheaper than paying a daily train fare for a bicycle as well as for himself. Buying a car was out of the question.

But the two-bicycle man did not like his job. The High School students were not sufficiently challenging. He would rather have had their minds to work with when they were able to argue back at him. He plodded on, laying a foundation of history and art, returning by train and two bicycles to his flat and his wife. Anky continued her job as secretary in the psychosomatic department of Amsterdam Hospital till six weeks before the baby was born, then she allowed herself a little rest.

On July 15th 1950, a message came to Hans between classes; it was a message he had been expecting. He reached for his pipe and began to fill it. "Well, I have a son."

Enormous thoughts swung round in his mind. He was a father to a new personality; what his father had once been to him. He regarded the thoughts gravely before filing them away. He glanced shyly at the members of faculty who were congratulating him; they expected him to get excited about it, but why? After all, babies had been born before. It was new for him but commonplace for the human race. Rookmaaker rammed more tobacco into his pipe and rammed his thoughts back into his current study of Gauguin.

Naturally the child would be named Henderik, the third in three generations. Hans visited his wife and son to bring them home from the hospital, then went back out of the door.

"Where are you going?" the new mother wanted to know.

"Back to study."

Anky was furious and said so.

The Rookmaaker son was baptised on July 30th in the parents' Gereformeerdekerk in South Amsterdam. During the next weeks a stream of friends came to the flat, peering at the tiny, blue-eyed baby and showering presents on the happy mother. All the usual things were said, "He has your eyes—your nose—his father's intent look."

When everyone had gone, Hans the father went to stand beside the cradle. How could one have a relationship with such a tiny person? It seemed a contradiction in terms: a human being who could neither speak, argue nor reason. Yet Anky seemed to understand instinctively how to communicate with the child by cuddles and little songs. What was the one she sang about the little cat? "Poesje? *Miaou*. Kom! *Miaou*." Hennie and Dora had sung it to him long ago but he could not imagine himself repeating the sing-song words to this strange little creature that was his first-born son.

Hans held a cautious finger down to the cradle. A jerking baby fist moved against it, more by accident than by decision. The fist opened and closed like a vice round his finger. Strange. Hans sighed. Maybe in six or seven years he and his son could begin to be friends.

He knew vaguely that he should create a friendly relationship with his students too. It was expected of a High School teacher that he should be available for casual chit-chat after class though Hans never seemed able to talk that way. Of course, he thought, he would buy a box of *cookjes* and hand them round. The students would eat the *cookjes* and they could chat together. He enjoyed the imaginary scene and made a note to remind himself to buy a box of *cookjes* in the lunch hour. He bought it and put it neatly away in the class cupboard with his files and future work plans.

A month went by and when Hans was tidying the cupboard in preparation for the holidays he came upon something that had nothing to do with his studies. *Cookjes?* Oh, of course, he had been going to use them to make friends with. He opened the box and tasted one, feeling a little foolish in the empty classroom. The *cookjes* were stale. Ruefully Hans dumped the box into the wastepaper basket and returned to his notebooks where the outline of his thesis on synthetist art theory was taking shape.

Anky knew he was not content with the job but she did what she could, keeping the household ticking over smoothly and plucking the crawling young Hansje out of his father's filing drawers. After the baby was born the Government had helped the little family to find a three room flat in the "not too good" south of Amsterdam. After a little while there they moved again, across the street into a better home. Rookmaaker's Amsterdam bicycle was parked in the front hall at night and on weekends. Anky, with a baby and the shopping in her arms and a second baby in her belly, squeezed past it in and out of the front door.

On Sunday evenings they had friends in to talk and, with Hans' enthusiasm being what it was, the talk became regular Sunday evening Bible Studies. Their friends, mostly church people, were taught by their church from books of theology and doctrine and prepared catechism lessons. Hans led them to Scripture itself. For some it was the first time they had read it for themselves. In youth groups they had been used to preparing a short epilogue on some Christian theme but their sources of information were theological books. Hans encouraged them to go to the original source.

"They were very good at their doctrine," said Anky as she remembered those evenings, "Hans learnt from them. Those Reformed young people could talk and talk about it. But they had not learned just to read the Bible. That's why they wanted to come to us. And Hans being a High School teacher, made him a respectable person to be teaching."

Their Reformed church friends regarded the young Rookmaaker couple as a little unusual (maybe it was the influence of their American friends) but at least they were regular in church attendance and kept a respectable home. There were rumours, though, that their observance of the Sabbath was not all that it should be. Hans had been seen coming out of an art gallery on a Sunday afternoon. One of the church elders remarked later, "Rookmaaker never knew what it was like to be really Reformed."

"Here is an interesting thing to happen," Hans showed Anky a letter, "I am invited to speak on art at a local church meeting."

"I wonder if they will like what you have to say?"

"We will see. It is good that they at least want to learn something about it."

They committed the invitation to God, praying in detail for specific things. Their Reformed friends preferred to ask for general blessings on their lives, regarding shopping-list prayer with grave suspicion. There had been some heated arguments between the Rookmaakers and members of their congregation. Was it not lowering God to expect Him to be concerned with little things like the price of a second-hand bicycle? On the other hand, was it not a step towards deism to say God could not be concerned? The Rookmaakers persisted in their own ideas. Since neither had been brought up in the Reformed tradition, they felt no shame at being different and their lack of background made that difference excusable. It was not that they were rebelling against the accepted norms of Calvinist upbringing; they had never had them in the first place.

Hans returned home late in the evening of the art talk at the church. Anky served him a late night glass of wine and waited for a suitable moment before she asked, "How was it?" She had learned that too many direct questions at the wrong time closed him up like a mussel.

He leant back in his chair, reliving the scene at the church hall. "It went well, of course. They had never had anyone to speak on the subject before so it was just as well they began with someone who knew something about it. One man said the subject was too worldly. I don't think I will be invited back." He frowned.

"Did they understand what you told them?"

"They thought art was a sinful thing."

"Well, that is no surprise. You knew they felt that way before you went."

"Before—yes. But I could not get through to them."

"Did you show them slides?"

"Yes, but their minds were closed. They could not receive them. They are good Christians but when it comes to art they have made a decision to be blind."

Hans Rookmaaker was to fight against that blindness for much of his subsequent life. The battle-lines of his ministry were being drawn for him. Time and again he would be brought up short against the idea that Christians ought not to soil their redeemed hands with paint or greasepaint. He fought against the attitude, insisting that a Christian was called to redeem his culture, turning it godwards any way he could, with words, music, architecture, movement, poetry, paint or clay. "The truth of God and the structures of godliness can speak out through every form of human art. We must learn how to do this so our contemporaries can *see* the Gospel."

He took these ideas to people who had reduced the Christian life to a proper ordering of catechism class and proper behaviour on the Sabbath. Immovable tradition was hit hard by irresistible force. All over Amsterdam, in the small world of Reformed churchmanship, you could hear the crunch.

"There is no criticism of culture in the Bible. Solomon had people from the pagan world to help him build the Temple. The people were always reminded not to follow pagan gods, but that was something different. They could make use of skills and workmanship to make their Temple beautiful for the Lord. They were not to be cut off from surrounding nations in that way. If we reject culture we are just like the Cynics of the ancient world; like Diogenes in his tub."

As months went by he spoke in church groups, in women's groups and in suburban coffee mornings, learning how to reach adult minds. By being faced with uncomprehending and sometimes hostile audiences, he honed his lecture style till he could cope with almost anyone. One young wife who heard him in those days said, "He spoke so simply he put me off. It wasn't till later I realised he had to speak simply because he thought so deep."

Rookmaaker met people who appeared to love Reform

theology more than they loved Christ, implying that all things had moved closer to truth since Calvin. He gave them no peace. "You say the Reformation brought in good things? Yes, it brought in good things but look at what else; there is now a dichotomy between the spiritual and the everyday world. We say nowadays that a thing is *either* spiritual *or* it is real. What do we mean by that word 'real'? The things of the spirit are just as real as wood or stone. There is beauty, there are angels; these are real. On the other hand the material things are filled with deep, deep meaning, so a picture or a wedding ring is not just a material object but something much, much deeper. To separate creation like modern man does is an impoverishment of life.

"There is a confusion in your mind between culture and worldliness. You have a little excuse for this but only a little one; this confusion has been going on for twenty centuries.

"Of course we are not at home among people who have said 'No' to their Maker and Saviour but we are at home in this created world. There is no separation between spirit and matter. The tragedy of modern man began with the Reformation." Later he dared to say that many of the problems of British and American Evangelicals sprang from their tendency to pietism, and that that pietism had come from the separation of reality as it had been developed by the Puritans.

One of the things he had to think through was the reason for his own career. Art history was an unlikely tool for evangelism. What then was its use? "Is art history a hobby?" he was asked.

"Yes, all scholarship is a hobby. Plato had a beautiful definition of scholarly work. He said, 'All scholarship is born out of curiosity.' We are very curious to know what is there, how it is made, why it is made like this. These questions lead to discoveries and discoveries open eyes.

"Art history, like art itself, is not a function of anything. It is something of its own with a meaning of its own, just as a tree has its own meaning. A tree has been created by God and it's beautiful. It doesn't need to have any self-justification. It's there because it's there and we can say 'Thank you' for it.

"It is not standing on a little island, cut off from everything else, but it is tied in with many other things in the world. A tree is important in the ecological cycles of this world. It is made for the cows to lay under and have shadow; its branches the birds can be sitting on; it produces oxygen. When the tree is old we can use it to make wooden things. There are many ways the tree is important but we can never say the *reason* God made the tree was, let's say, to be branches for shading the cows, or for the birds to sit on. To say this, you make the tree too little.

"A tree is always more than any of its functions, because it has its own intrinsic value and meaning. So with art history and so with such a thing as marriage. It is there because it is there; a part of reality and a part of our life. If we say a thing has only value as a tool for evangelism, we become functionalist, or utilitarian people. We make the subject too small and we make ourselves too small."

Late in the evenings Hans would return home where Anky listened to his sorrow. "Oh, if only they could understand. They have made the Christian life so limited. They have made God so small. If only I could help them to see."

He had begun his study of art history as an ego trip, wanting to be the master guide along a path that was new to his Reformed contemporaries. Now compassion had moved alongside and was to travel with him for the rest of his life.

As time passed Rookmaaker tried to make his teaching similar to that of Solomon's *Book of Proverbs* in which there is instruction in wisdom to enlarge the understanding. A student of his last years said, "He did not so much tell you things as make you reflect on the nature of things."

He tested many of his ideas on Francis Schaeffer, enjoying his friendship with the American Presbyterian as much as he enjoyed any relationship of his life. He admired the pastor for his ability to get on with many kinds of people. Hans, the Son of the Resident, felt an occasional pang of ineffectiveness but he brushed it aside; what was the value of striking up a friendship with a road sweeper unless the man was able to talk intelligently about Descartes or Monet? He felt at home among University students and remained with them. In spite of countless visits to the Amsterdam Rijksmuseum he never got to know the museum guards by name. He did not look down on them; it was as though they were not there.

The Rookmaakers stayed in close, prayerful contact with their American friends and when the Revd. and Mrs. Schaeffer set up their chalet home as an open discussion ground for agnostics in 1954, the Rookmaakers followed the situation with interest. In 1955 they spent six weeks there with their children. The legalistic tendency of their church was weighing on them; it seemed so much of the Christian life had to do with negatives. High in the Alps they asked their questions and regained their vision from this pastor from Philadelphia and his wife.

"I did not become a Christian through their influence," Anky remembered, "but I do not think I would have stayed in the Christian way without it."

In 1958 Hans and Anky became formally connected with the Schaeffers' community as Dutch representatives. In practice their lives were unchanged; they still had Bible studies in their home where they saw young people once a week or a fortnight. But now they felt free to send an occasional person to Switzerland, if they thought he could be better helped in a Christian residential situation.

When Hans and Francis met in the Netherlands they walked and talked for hours, thrashing their beliefs and ideas back and forth over the issue of pre- versus a-millennianism. Schaeffer fought for a literal thousand-year reign of Christ on earth while Hans found that view too simplistic and said so. They agreed to disagree. There was much more in Scripture to talk about.

Hans taught Francis about art. Letters began to flow between the Netherlands and Switzerland, often containing a cutting or a translation from a contemporary journal that dealt with some issue of culture. They interpreted things differently, as thinkers will. Years later, after Schaeffer had published a small book about art, Rookmaaker confessed to a friend that he had not read the book. "Schaeffer and I are such good friends. I would rather not find I disagree with him over this."

Hans had left his High School job after two years and had gone to Leiden University as art teacher. After some talking, he and a lady member of the Art History Institute faculty agreed to exchange jobs. She became a High School teacher, getting more salary, while Hans became the Netherlands equivalent of what the English call Assistant Professor. He got less salary but more time to study.

University students began to drop in at the Rookmaakers' with the church people on Sunday evenings. Hans, pipe in hand, expounded his way through *The Epistle to the Romans*, answering questions with uncompromising toughness. His listeners, being equally Dutch, responded with equal toughness. Arguments heated up but at the end of the evening, everyone remained friends.

"I still think you are quite wrong about justification," said a philosophy student, as he put on his bicycle clips and muffler ready to leave.

"Never mind. I think you have it wrong too."

"Will you come back next week, Gerrit?" asked Anky.

"Yes, of course." The young man turned back to Hans, "I like to talk to someone who has not always been Reformed. You are not giving me what you have learnt in catechism class as a child. You have arrived somewhere by your own mind. I think that is good."

"So. I hope you can arrive there too."

When the last guests had gone, Hans and Anky tidied up the coffee cups together. "So strange," said Hans, "they have so much theology but they have not looked at the Bible straight to see what it says. Instead of me learning from them, they learn from me."

Anky kissed him goodnight before he went to his study for the next two hours. As art critic for the Calvinist publication, *Trouw*, he visited art exhibitions, good and bad, all over the Netherlands, fitting publishing deadlines into his weekly teaching schedule and studies for his thesis.

In spite of the amount of work (or maybe because of it) it was a happy time of his life. In the family album there is a photo of Hans Rookmaaker at this time. A strong profile is crowned with a bush of brown hair standing high on his head and clipped tightly about the ears. The roguish grin is only a little more mature than when he was a teenager. He is wearing baggy, 1950s trousers with pleats at the waist and his shirt sleeves are held up with sleeve bands. The picture was snapped at an open-air Bible study. Hans seems to be enjoying himself immensely.

He wrote *Synthetist Art Theories* in 1959, completing it in three months. He had all the material in his files and in his mind; he had been studying for it, all told, for eleven years.

Before Anky went to bed that night after the Bible Study, she peeped in to check on the two sleeping children, Hans and baby Kees. They were tucked up in American sleeping suits that a friend of Mrs. Schaeffer had sent from the States. Now that a smaller salary was coming in, every little helped. Before she slept, Anky knelt before God, committing to Him every detail of their family needs.

"Hans' studies went on for years," she remembered later, "and we had to manage somehow with two small children and with all those students to feed. It was not easy."

CHAPTER ELEVEN

The Family Rookmaaker

As THE TWO children passed through babyhood, the Rookmaakers' home life became more settled. A better salary enabled Hans and Anky to save and move to a house in Diemen, an outpost of suburbia floating in green fields to the east of Amsterdam. Their end-of-the-row terrace house was built in the usual Dutch pattern with living and dining rooms opening out front to back and a kitchen to the side. There was a minute garden in front and a minute garden at the back where a pet tortoise roamed under the leaves.

The Chinese vase of Hans' childhood days was transferred to its place in the new living room and the carved archway of Indonesian wood was hung on the dining room wall. Upstairs there was more room for books and filing drawers. Hans buried himself in his new study.

There were three children in the family now: Hansje, Kees and Marleen. Theodora Rookmaaker showered presents on them all, including a high-priced portrait of her eldest grandchild, painted by a fashionable artist. She never understood her own son's way of life, "Are you *still* studying, dear?"

Hans and Anky thanked her for the painting and hung it where she could see it during her visits to Diemen. The painting was as uninteresting as a tinted photograph. Between themselves, the young parents made no secret of the fact that they would rather have had the money.

One Sunday evening, shortly after they had moved to Diemen, Papa Rookmaaker decided it was time to take his eldest son's religious instruction in hand. "Hansje, come to my study. There is a little book that I want we read together."

The seven-year-old followed his father into the room that he had always regarded as a kind of holy place. Rookmaaker fitted the child onto his knee and opened a book on the parables of Jesus.

"Now you see, Hansje, the Good Samaritan represents . . ." (then came the explanation) "and the traveller represents . . ." (another explanation). The father bent his head round to look into the child's solemn face. "Do you think you understand?"

"Er, yes, Father."

"Good. Then we continue." After a while he asked the child again, "Do you think you understand?"

"Yes, Father."

Week after week, Sunday supper was followed by the scene in the study. Parable after parable was thoroughly explained and the child nodded obediently and said "Yes, Father," when he was asked. One evening, after the child had been allowed to slip off his lap and be tucked into bed by Anky, Rookmaaker sat alone with the little booklet. He had chosen it with care; the doctrinal content was sound. He sighed, thumbing through its pages. The interpretation of the parables was clear enough to him and he had tried to put it into simple language. He put the booklet away in the appropriate place on his shelves. Maybe when the child was older they could try again.

"I really did try to take in what he was telling me," remembered the adult son, "but I think he was giving me a simplified version of Dooyeweerdian philosophy." With the perception of a child, young Hansje noticed that when his brother and sister reached the comparable age, they were never summoned to the study on Sunday evenings and the little booklet on the parables never reappeared.

Hans, Kees and Marleen got used to hearing their father say things like, "Children do not become really interesting till they are eleven years or so," and "I am not interested in young children. I find them quite a nuisance."

They saw him, briefly, in the evenings before he vanished into his study to work on some dissertation or MS. He was only theirs on Sunday afternoons and those times were joyous. Papa Rookmaaker settled Anky to relax after the Sunday meal, then he and the children took off on their fleet of bicycles. When Marleen was too small to ride her own, she went on the back of her father's bicycle on a special seat. Those Sunday rides took them to parks, to art galleries and often to Amsterdam's Artis Zoo.

"Do you know that your *Opa* [Grandfather] once discovered a new kind of frog and the frog was named after him?"

"You already told us, Papa."

"Papa, Kees wants to look at the rhinos! Can we all go and see the rhinos?"

"Papa, look at the tiger looking at me! Did God give him stripes so he could hide in the trees?"

"Yes, as I told you last week. And do you see that the stripes are not only to make him hide but also to be beautiful?"

"Yes, yes, I see!"

"Papa, can we go and find the frog that is called *Opa*?"

While Anky took a well-deserved Sunday afternoon rest, Rookmaaker and his children found happiness in all creatures great and small. They cycled home for supper and bed, in summer daylight or through the dusk of spring and autumn evenings; Papa Rookmaaker with his large feet planted firmly on the pedals, his children following on their small bikes like a row of ducklings.

The children, who spent their Sunday afternoons at the Zoo, would grow up to echo many a student whom their father had patiently led through an art museum: "He taught me to know what I was seeing. He taught me to look."

The children remember their father as being enthusiastic about mechanical things, always tinkering with loudspeakers and finding the best way to put something on tape. Record collectors and jazz buffs from other parts of the Netherlands came to share tapes and early-issue records. The children grew up listening to the same jazz piece played ten times in a row by different musicians while father and the visitors discussed interpretation and style.

113

He loved to explain things to his children: sound waves, jazz styles and machinery.

"He explained the workings of a car at least ten times to me," remembered Hans the son, "but I never got it right."

Hans the father did not always get it right either, becoming frustrated by the innate perversity of machinery. The Rookmaaker car was second-hand and subject to fainting fits in the middle of the road. The family bank balance had to wait several years before he could afford to buy a spruce Mercedes and even that was second-hand.

Once the children tried their father's patience to the limit. Visitors had come for a meal and it went on longer than usual with much discussion about finances for a community centre in the Netherlands. The children became bored. The grown-ups moved into the living room and the children, with their toys, were relegated to the back.

"We began by making small noises," the elder son remembered, "then bigger noises. After a while we saw that the grown-ups were praying. We children started yelling and shrieking to attract attention. I was the oldest so I suppose I really was the one to blame."

As the meeting drew to a close, Hansje wriggled through the crowd at the front door and hid in an upstairs cupboard. There he waited for what seemed like hours for a ten-year-old. "Finally the last guest left and my father rushed upstairs and took me from the cupboard. That was the only time he hit me."

Sunday worship was one of the things that was taken seriously in the family, though the Rookmaakers did not conform to the life-style of their church in all things. A strictly Reformed father in those days was not supposed to take his children to the Zoo on Sunday. *Trouw,* the publication for which Hans did the art reviews, did not report sporting events if they were played on the Christian Sabbath. Dutch Calvinism tended more to Sabbath observance than to Sabbath joy.

On Sunday mornings the family was respectable; sitting in a row in their pew, sucking the traditional peppermints when the long sermon began. Hans Rookmaaker only succumbed to the national peppermint habit once and that was when the visiting preacher was a man of elaborate gestures and dramatic style.

"You were trying not to laugh, Papa! That's why you asked for Kees' bag of peppermints!" his children accused him in the car afterwards.

Papa Rookmaaker denied it absolutely. Anky, with laughter in her eyes, shushed the children and let her husband save face on the journey home.

"Father, Dhr. Klaus says it is a sin to play sports on Sunday; can I play tennis this afternoon?"

"Why not, Hansje?"

"Is it all right, then?"

"Why not? You have attended Christian worship, have you not? Then take your Sabbath rest in the way that is appropriate for you, in energetic sport. But when you go to the tennis courts, walk round by the other road as you will not pass by the houses of some of our church friends. They will not grieve over what they cannot see."

Hansje, clad in tennis togs, trotted nervously through side streets to the tennis courts on Sunday afternoons, feeling as if the eye of every neighbour was upon him.

The Rookmaakers ploughed a steady furrow through Reform-norms, spending their Sunday spare time at zoos, art galleries, cinemas, picnics, bike rides, anything their family heart desired. On Monday mornings Rookmaaker would descend to a silent breakfast, morose and distant, his mind thrust back into his books.

Anky was a natural morning person, rising fresh as a lark at six-thirty to make sandwich lunches for her school-age children. Hans was a natural night-owl who could study till the small hours and sleep as soon as his head touched the pillow. In the morning he would shuffle downstairs, silent as an oyster, touchy as a bear, unwilling to be spoken to till eleven a.m. At eight a.m. he would select a record with care and play it as an audible barrier to conversation while he sipped his coffee and ate his lightly-stirred fried egg.

Once Anky had to break the no-talking rule to remind him of a family dental appointment that had had to be changed.

He harrumphed something into the dregs of his coffee and left for the University. When he returned that evening he slumped into his chair, petulant as a child. "You really should not have spoken to me seriously first thing in the morning. It quite ruined my day."

"He never would talk," said Anky, "He could not chat about little ordinary things. Philosophical discussion, yes, he could do that. But when you have a wife and children you cannot always be carrying on a philosophical discussion. You must sometimes speak of other things."

In 1961 Rookmaaker was sent to the U.S. on a grant from the Netherlands government to study methods of art teaching in Boston University and various colleges in New York State. When he came home his most enthusiastic memories were not of American art teaching but of the Black music he had heard.

He attended an all-Black church and got himself invited to a jazz-session in a church hall, the first white man ever to attend. A Dutch pastor said of Rookmaaker that "he had his own kind of emotionalism, one that not everyone could understand". For a man who rejoiced in rational thought and cool Calvinist worship, it seemed strange that Black American praise, free-spirited and full of heart, should have the power to touch something in him.

He met Mahalia Jackson, and there are no prizes for guessing what they talked about. He admired the singer's Christian approach to her work. At home he loved to play her song "I'm gonna move on up a little higher", dwelling on the words,

> Soon one evening, I'm going home to live on high;
> Soon as my feet strike Zion, gonna lay down my heavy burden,
> Put on my robe in glory, going home and tell my story . . .
> Gonna move on up a little higher, gonna meet the Lily of the Valley,
> Gonna move on up a little higher, gonna feast with the Rose of Sharon . . .
> It will be always howdy, howdy and never goodbye.

"That is the Christian attitude towards death," Rookmaaker told his friends. "I would like that record to be played at my funeral."

While he was in America, Anky kept the household going and waited anxiously for the transatlantic phone-call her husband had promised. It came through at last.

"Anky?"

"Yes, your voice is quite clear. Talk fast, it must be so expensive."

"I do not know what to say. I am all right."

"Well, where are you staying? What is the American food like? Which colleges have you visited? Did you meet the Schaeffers' friends?"

"Er, hmm . . . well, it is very cold here. What is the weather like in the Netherlands?"

"Oh, what does it matter what the weather is like in the Netherlands? We want to know about you and your trip!"

"Oh. Well. It is er, it is very cold here. And it was cold yesterday."

Years later, when trips to the U.S. had become regular events in Rookmaaker's lecture ministry, his growing family learnt to expect nothing more from the transatlantic calls.

"It's father phoning from Ithaca," said one child, handing the receiver to his mother.

"Huh," said another child, barely glancing up from her homework, "another weather report."

When he was home and Anky's patience was stretched to the limit, Hans was all husbandly concern, treating her as though she were delicate porcelain. He insisted she rest while he did the washing up himself.

He loved to potter about the garden and the house where he exercised his mind over the small necessities of where to put a clothes line or a picture hook. He tied a teaspoon on the radiator pipe that rose from the Diemen kitchen to the upstairs and told Anky to bang it when she wanted him down for a meal.

Family holidays were a disaster. For several years Anky tried renting a cottage in the woodland near Amsterdam.

She took her housework with her and tried to give the children a nice time, while Hans itched to be back in his books (if he did not actually take them with him). Enforced idleness and country rambles for a week at a time were not his idea of a holiday. He could not sit still and look at the clouds.

As the children grew a little older, Anky tried taking them all to Ireland. The Rookmaakers loved the rolling green landscapes of Southern Ireland but things were not smooth with Hans around.

"I have been consulting the guidebooks," he would announce at breakfast, to a tableful of groaning relatives, "There is a historic castle twenty miles away and then off in the other direction a house of particularly interesting architectural style. There is also a museum that I wish to go to. Now if we begin after breakfast—"

"Oh, no!" "Why can't we just do nothing for a day?" "Potter!" "Sit in the sun!" "Have a holiday!"

"Very well, we can relax today if you wish it. Then to-morrow—"

"What? All day racing about looking at things?"

"No. Not all day," the paterfamilias corrected them with dignity, "We need not start till about ten-fifteen or ten-thirty and we will be back here at four-thirty or four-forty-five. Now, you cannot say that is all day." They fussed at him and finally learned to bear with him. He could not relax. There was too much in the world to learn.

He had an almost totally blind spot for fiction. He could not see the explorative side of the form, nor could he get involved in lives that did not exist or situations that had not occurred. The only fictional books that reached his mind were C. S. Lewis' *The Great Divorce* and *The Chronicles of Narnia*. He caught Lewis' vision of progression in heaven and loved to quote from the seventh Narnia story "farther up and farther in". But he was frustrated at having discovered Lewis too late to arrange a meeting between them.

Sport, the relaxation of many good minds, was as incomprehensible to him as a novel. His son tried to interest him in a televised football match. "Even if you know nothing of the rules of the game, Father, at least you can see that one side or the other has the ball."

"Yes, I can see that, but what is the purpose? I am tired of the camera going from side to side. Ach, you watch it; I have other things to do."

In the autumn of 1966 he and Anky opened their home for Sunday evening Bible studies in Diemen, and soon word spread among Reformed people that it was a good place to bring unbelieving friends. Anky counted up to fifty people sitting on her living room floor and overflowing into the hall. One visitor was Aagje, a nurse from Friesland, with red-gold hair. Hans the son seemed to like sitting beside her.

Inevitably word of the Bible studies spread on the grapevine of art students. One of them introduced himself to Hans and Anky and told them he had been studying art at Basel. "But I am ready to stop, I think. There seems no purpose in it. They show us how to look at everything in the world as though it is machinery, just lines and blocks and planes. That may be all right when you are painting machinery, you understand, but when you learn to look at a human being that way it is not good."

Marc remembered years later that Rookmaaker's teaching about art irritated him at first. "He made you think about things, but he didn't fill in all the details."

By 1967 he knew who he wanted his teacher to be and he switched from Basel to the Free University of Amsterdam. The Swiss art teaching had been based on Bauhaus principles, fragmenting the world into blocks and planes. Rookmaaker was different: he talked about organic unity and freedom within form.

"I will tell you how I approach art," said Rookmaaker, when he was asked about his methods, "I do not see a picture merely as an expression of an artist and his emotions at the time of painting, but as a philosophy that he expresses. I do not ask, 'What can I find out of this artist's private thoughts?' but 'What does the artist tell me about the world?' "

"After two and a half years," Marc remembered, "his

teaching changed me. That is good because if you immediately change with a new teacher you do not know if it is really yourself or if you only make a copy of someone else's point of view. Rookmaaker preferred someone to wrestle with ideas rather than just to say 'Yes, you are right.' "

When Marc was married in 1969, Rookmaaker gave the wedding guests at the Haarlem Town Hall ceremony a ten-minute talk on Christian marriage. It was an unusual wedding gift but well received.

Under the influence of Rookmaaker's teaching, the artist's work began to show a slow shift. A series of photographs of the Eiffel Tower included a human figure standing among the network of girders. After having seen the world through Cubist eyes, it was the first recognition in his work that the world was more than nuts and bolts. As he passed into Christian belief, his paintings passed into a portrayal of the created world. It was not the surface reality of a mindless photograph but something that showed the living reality of what God has made.

"He became like a father to me," said Marc of his teacher. "Not in the emotional way but in the way he prepared me for the world. I learned to look at the world as a Christian should look. There is beauty and there is sin but there is no longer a sense of threat. I would have given up art if it had not been for Rookmaaker."

Others found him a similar help. Rookmaaker talked for long hours with Wim Rietkerk during his studies at Kampen Theological College, helping the young man with questions he himself had wrestled with years before. Wim spent his summers at the community in Switzerland, helping to dig vegetable gardens and meeting other theological students from America and England. Often he returned to question Rookmaaker again on some point he thought he had resolved.

"It does not matter if Jonah was historical or not." Rookmaaker bravely declared during one Bible study in Diemen.

Hans van Seventer once took him to task about those

120

Bible Studies. "You should allow more time for discussion. They do not want your voice all the time."

Hans, a fellow Dutchman, could dare to be *brutaal* with Rookmaaker. The word means forthright to the point of being cocky. Rookmaaker was often accused of being *brutaal*, but this time he took the rebuke thoughtfully. "Discussion during the study? Yes, I see. Well, I will try it next time."

"He would work at it for a bit," Hans van Seventer remembered later, "then he would be so full of what he wanted to say that the monologue would wash over the room again."

The Rookmaakers became like second parents to Hans and his American wife, JoAnn, inviting them for a meal once a week to talk and pray together.

In spite of his monologue style of teaching the Bible, Rookmaaker was capable of thinking freely around the edges of Calvinist orthodoxy. He spoke of "central theology"; that place where all who love Christ can agree in peace. He visited Kampen Theological College, staying up late to talk; more like a student himself than a professor.

"We must not be afraid of new ideas or of non-Reformed ideas. The Catholics say certain things about their Mass and we cannot meet our minds together, but we can still learn about God from one another."

"What about purgatory?" asked a Calvinist student, probably used to hearing diatribes against Tetzel.

Rookmaaker puffed his pipe and thought. "For myself, I believe a Christian goes straight to the presence of God. But I can see that another view could fit quite well into the Christian framework. Those who believe like this are also my brothers in the Lord and I am a brother to them."

Another question: what about church affiliation?

"Yes, of course we must relate to individual Christians and to one particular church but ultimately our church affiliation is a smaller thing than Christian fellowship."

As his three children grew up he let them think for themselves. On the advice of the eldest child, the two younger Rookmaakers had been sent to secular schools, learning to fight for the right to hold Christian views among classmates whose moral standards were against God. From the age of twelve, all three children had been expected to sit in on discussions with students at their Diemen home. Most of the talk went over their heads but they saw how Christian truth could stand up to reasoned debate. When they reached their own age of questioning, they knew they could bring their questions home without fear.

"He always trusted his children," said a family friend. "He let them listen to the hardest rock music without condemning it. In fact he used to listen with them and talk about it so they knew what they were hearing."

One of his children grew up to be an English teacher, another studied the history of music, another became a published authority of the captive rhinosceri of Europe during the last four hundred and fifty years. Hans the younger gave Hans the elder a lot of material for the father's lecture "Beat, Rock and Protest" with its recorded illustrations by names that have now passed into pop music history: the Beatles, Leonard Cohen, Bob Dylan, Simon and Garfunkel.

After a while Hans the elder became an elder in more ways than one. The grey-haired churchman was asked to stand for election as Elder in his congregation. It was an appointment that was suggested with some trepidation from the church members. Rookmaaker was staunchly Calvinist, but what would he get up to next in his thinking and teaching? Elders were noted for their steady, dependable qualities; this man had proved himself as dependable as a captive rhino rasping against the bars of his cage.

CHAPTER TWELVE

Adjustments

HE WAS ELECTED as Elder to serve for the regulation four years. He respected the post, only kicking over the traces at church meetings to ask awkward questions about unquestioned traditional ways.

Dhr. Brouwer, a fellow Elder, said of him, "Rookmaaker had a totally other tradition behind him, or I should say no tradition. We all had the heritage of Reformed churchmanship but also I think there were disadvantages. You see, before the war, the Reformed church was a closed group and wanted to remain so. We were still living in the time of Abraham Kuyer, the Prime Minister who died in 1920. Rookmaaker came onto the scene freshly. Seeing and hearing him, some of us felt we were missing something. He learnt, I hope, from us and we learnt from him.

"To come together for praying, for example, that we didn't know in our tradition. We found it a little overdone. Oh yes, we pray several times a day, and when we have an assembly to debate, we begin and end with prayer. But we have not a meeting for prayer only. We can appreciate this but at the same time it is strange to us."

Rookmaaker's apologetics were also new to his Reformed contemporaries. To him nothing was taken for granted. Everything, even the existence of God, was a subject of careful debate before moving to the next step. But his special forte in the church was asking questions.

"This way of doing things may have been right once, but is it right now? Is this way of life part of the central circle in which the essential things of Christianity are held, or is it in the outer circle where ways of life may alter from age to age? Or is it even beyond the outer circle of Christian life?"

Dhr. Brouwer reminded him that there is nothing beyond the outer circle but that, finally, every action and area of life is under the hand of God.

Rookmaaker accepted the correction but kept to his theoretical inner and outer circle concept, using it to distinguish what must be believed from what may be debated.

"As an Elder, Rookmaaker questioned why we are doing such and such a thing for a century. Someone known to be in public sins, for example, is traditionally turned back from the Communion table by an Elder standing at each side, taking turns. Rookmaaker asked us 'Why?' We talked about this and came to the opinion that it has sense in organising. But some things had nearly lost their meaning for us through tradition.

"Rookmaaker was a man who could come with open eyes and wonderful face and was asking such questions. We had to dig deep in our heads to find our answers. We never had such questions before."

After serving four years, and with the traditional two years off, Rookmaaker was elected to serve as Elder again. One thing a fellow member of the congregation noticed: when he was appointed to the proud post of Professor at the Free University of Amsterdam, no-one was ever allowed to call him Professor in church.

As a man known for his Calvinism, Rookmaaker was asked to be a paid member of the National Board of Film Censors. Several times a year he viewed questionable films and gave his Christian opinion as to whether they should be allowed in ordinary (i.e. non-club) cinemas. He turned down several *Kung Fu* films in which a thin storyline is spread like sauce over mindless violence. But he approved the showing of *Fritz the Cat*, the California-made sex cartoon, because it was honest about the sadness of permissive life.

At this stage of his ministry, it was fashionable for people to talk about and be involved in "the new morality" and "the permissive life-style". Rookmaker delighted to tackle the issues in a Christian fashion. By keeping in close contact with the student generation he, more than other middle-aged Professors, knew what was going on in their minds. Attitudes to morality changed but his vision of reality did not flinch. Somehow he managed to weld the separate interests of his life into one: St. Paul and Rubens and Jelly-Roll Morton, oriental food and Negro music, Calvinist church Eldership and *Fritz the Cat*.

In the 1960s Rookmaaker appeared to be the only man in the Netherlands to combine art history knowledge with a university background, a PhD and outspoken Christian belief. The Vrije Universiteit (the VU) offered him their Art History chair. Rookmaaker gave his inaugural speech in 1965 following lines of thought that he had begun to map out through Dooyeweerd and with the help of Mekkes over twenty years before. Then he was plunged into five years of hard work as he established himself and his department.

After that he faced a shift of admissions policy that bowed to the Government's pressure of democratisation in the Universities. Before World War II, further education was for a favoured twenty-five per cent. Now it was rising to eighty per cent. With not enough university places available, students went where they were sent. Instead of a select ten new students who had chosen the VU for its Christian perspective, Rookmaaker was faced with twenty new-comers, some of whom introduced a Marxist tone to the department. For the man who had arrived at Christian convictions by hard interior questioning it was a bitter disappointment. Precious lecture time had to be spent in basic Christian apologetics instead of in building up the faith and deepening the perception of believing students. His reaction to the Leftist newcomers was described as "more spontaneous than diplomatic".

The democratisation of university life did not come easily to him at first. "He enjoyed the role of Worthy Professor," said a member of the art department who knew him in those days. "He expected respect and when he didn't get enough he tried to enforce it. In the student world of the 1960s, it was the worst game to play. As time went on though, I was amazed at how much he did manage to adjust."

Adjustment did not come easily and there were complaints in the small department: "Rookmaaker spends too much time with pet students and with foreigners" (i.e. the non-Dutch). "He is not an administrator." "He spends too much time with work for that Swiss group." "You can go to alternate lectures; he repeats himself so much." "He claims it is new material but it isn't." "His approach to art is too speculative and too much involved with Bible philosophy."

Misunderstandings were mixed with valid criticism, for some of the complaints were justified, as some of a group of complaints usually are. Rookmaaker made an effort to change, going out of his way to strike up conversations with Dutch students in the coffee area on the eighth floor of the VU. He took a graduate excursion to Berlin in the autumn of 1975, visiting galleries in the East and West sectors, in Dresden and in Potsdam. His material was new; his gallery lectures were good. It was as though he drew power from the physical presence of the artist's work. Back at the VU he listened while an American and an Australian student patiently tried to explain why the difficulties had arisen, but some of the complaints were beyond his comprehension. "But what shall I do? What am I doing wrong?" There were tears in his eyes.

It was his English assistant who helped him over many rough spots, feeling like a buffer as many peacemakers do. Graham Birtwistle had first heard of Rookmaaker in 1965 from a Travelling Secretary for Inter-Varsity Fellowship in England (now called the University and Colleges Christian Fellowship).

"He's a Christian art historian," the Travelling Secretary had said, "Little chap with a round face and smokes a pipe. Looks like Harold Wilson."

Graham was not concerned with what the man looked like. A little later he came across a book that interested him in the library of Leicester College of Art where he was teaching art history. The book was *Synthetist Art Theories* and on the flyleaf blurb it was written that the author had been converted to Christ. Graham thought it was an unusual thing for an art historian to say. He stored the contents of the book in his mind, afterwards describing Rookmaaker's thesis as "the greatest single influence in turning me away from irrationalism".

In the summer of 1966, the young man from Accrington was visiting the Schaeffers' community in the Swiss Alps. A round middle-aged Dutchman walked into the chalet living room; he introduced himself as Hans Rookmaaker. Graham was surprised. He had not known that Rookmaaker knew the Schaeffers.

"My first impression," remembered Graham, "was that his tastes and interests were diametrically opposed to mine. Things that I liked—Abstract Expressionism for example—he couldn't stand. And he said so in no uncertain terms. But he'd obviously analysed the artists seriously. He wrote off people that my own thinking was orientated towards but he wrote them off with knowledge."

Graham and Rookmaaker went for a walk, strolling halfway round the mountain and back again. Graham spoke of subconscious influences in the work of Surrealists and Rookmaaker suggested that the subconscious did not exist.

"Man lived for centuries without this concept. Now that we have it, see how useful it is. We unload onto it all our guilts, saying 'It is my subconscious; I cannot help myself.' Maybe it does not exist after all, and we are more responsible than we dare to admit. But tell me, have you not studied the Dutch seventeenth-century artists or Dürer?"

"Frankly no, not seriously; I didn't feel they had anything to offer me. I think my mentality is more Abstract."

"So because they speak an unfamiliar language you refuse to listen?"

Rookmaaker spoke of a Calvinist view of reality as the most Christian view, because it opened up the idea of a world structured by the Creator for man's responsible use. Graham wondered aloud if there was a view that tried to escape from that created reality. For answer, Rookmaaker described the mind-set of the Symbolist Romantics of the late nineteenth century. Graham was conscious of a deep and lasting shock. He had attended Baptist Sunday School through his childhood and had had some of his later questions answered by people in Inter-Varsity Fellowship.

Now, hearing Rookmaaker describe the Symbolists, he thought, *"He's describing me."* He found his mind was not tuned to the Bible at all. There were layers of other influences that had to be rethought.

He returned to Leicester and lived for the next six months with an experience of dislodgement from traditional evangelical ways of living and thinking. Early in 1967 he wrote to the Professor asking he if could go to the Netherlands to study art history. He wanted to do a PhD Rookmaaker wrote encouraging letters back and explained the Dutch scholastic system. It did not tally with the British one and the standards were high. Graham would need a *doctoraal* (roughly the equivalent of an MA) before he worked on his dissertation. It had to be done.

"I was confronted by a mentality that I had to take seriously. But it was a challenge. There were new ideas to grasp. I realised I'd seen something new and I couldn't go back. When you've seen something like that you can't pretend it isn't there."

He achieved his post-graduate purpose in 1970 and beavered his way to a post of Assistant Professor in the small art history department of the VU, learning Dutch along the way. He and the Professor discovered a mutual interest in jazz.

The Wednesday seminars on Christianity and Art usually ended at the VU at eleven p.m. so Rookmaaker stayed overnight in Graham's cottage outside Amsterdam to be on time for the nine a.m. lecture the next day. The overnight arrangement had begun with two of his married students and when they left in 1976, and Graham moved into the cottage, he continued the tradition. Those late-night conversations with the Professor were times of good friendship; talk flowed from Dürer to Johnny Dodds to the design of the DC7s.

"It was usually around midnight when we poured the whiskey and put on the jazz records," Graham remembered.

Through the 1960s Rookmaaker adjusted to his students' changing world, reading Jack Kerouac and listening intelligently to the Rolling Stones. He quoted from Ginsberg's

Howl, and traced how the beat generation shifted from being beatific to being beaten down. He watched the Flower Children wither and heard the cry of the Permissive people as, bewildered and divorced, they scrabbled after the standards they had been too quick to throw away.

As the standards of the pagan world filtered down to the Reformed sub-culture a few years later, he saw that there were some confessing Christians among the bruised reeds. He expressed his sorrow over one case in a letter to a mutual friend:

"I have talked to the young man several times but have not had any chance to 'get through'. He is going to live with his new wife, even at this moment, as the other marriage is still not dissolved. He says he feels free. The problem is he sees no problem, and thinks this can be done *as* a Christian. He says he can do so as the Gospel gives him the freedom to do so—and his sins are forgiven.

"We are—were—shocked. And I'm still thinking how to deal with this. Also with the Christian group this is a real problem. Yesterday, in talking to him, I told him that—unless things drastically change—he is not seen any more as a Christian by me. I want to remain friends, but not within the Christian group."

He wrote further that Christian leadership should be taken from the young man, and the letter continued in sorrow, "He is not able to understand my view on these things. He is far gone. Christian discipleship—in the sense of church discipline—he does not accept in any way . . . It is all destructive. And negative . . . It makes me weep, really."

On another occasion he spoke to some of his students on the subject of marriage: "We may become a tiny island of monogamy in a free-love world, as a little museum of what was once,widespread. We should not be proud of our life-style or strive to be a sub-culture. We must never take the attitude 'we the in-crowd' but always keep contact with contemporaries."

He helped his Christian friends do their own counselling and the subject of immorality came up during one of his times with Hans and JoAnn and with Marc. He encouraged them to help people stand against the current wave of softness that could lead even professing Christians to change their marriage partners when the mood took them or if they did not feel mature enough to cope.

"God gives to everyone his gifts. Some may spend all their energy keeping their marriage together. Others may spend their life in other ways. In God's eyes it is the same value. Be glad with your own gifts. Tell people you cannot marry the wrong woman but you can live the wrong way with the woman you have married. It is in the little things, the flowers, the cups of coffee together, the little things of life that the Gospel makes a difference."

On the new Christian talking point of homosexuality he was firm. A tendency in this direction was a battle to be fought. "It may be that a Christian will have to fight this all his life but that is his calling before the Lord. As for us, we cannot judge another man's battle."

The sixties was the era of the Beautiful People when morals flowed as freely as the hair and to be over thirty was to be over the hill. In those days students became entranced by oriental teachers, sitting with naked navels and garlands of flowers. The most unlikely person to capture their attention was a middle-aged Dutchman who dressed like a bank manager and was built like Bilbo Baggins. Throughout the hippy sixties Hans Rookmaaker remained as uncompromisingly square as he always had been. He never sat on the floor, never took his shoes off in public; he always wore a suit and waistcoat and always had his hair cut short-back-and-sides.

He was proud of his English-made suits, bought off-the-peg during his holidays and with the trousers slightly shortened. His students at the VU teased him one day, "Do you ever wear anything else, Professor?"

"No. Always a suit and waistcoat."

"What about when you are pottering about in your garden?"

"Then I wear an old suit and waistcoat."

"Don't you ever go informal and wear a sweater?"

He looked down at his teddy-bear figure, then his impish brown eyes twinkled up at them, "Now, can you really imagine me in a sweater?"

As he passed into the fifth decade of his life there were dark circles under his eyes. His round cheeks sagged and his hair silvered. He wore reading glasses on a chain round his neck.

Friends reported seeing him rise to towering rages over small-mindedness and what he considered a wilful non-comprehension of the beauties of great art. When the charismatic movement became a talking point in the late sixties, he became very disturbed, his fear of irrationalism making him blind to what might be good in it. In his generation, the word Tongues was associated with back-street Pentecostalism, ranting and narrow and anti-art. He could not adjust to seeing it differently and on two occasions friends saw his fury almost deprive him of rational speech. Said a colleague, "He could be like a wild animal. You felt there was something there that was quite untamed."

"What made him angry," said a teacher from another country, "was anything that opposed his concept of the integral quality of Christianity. One of his fundamental objections to the charismatic movement was that he felt it denigrated matter and was pietistic. That was against everything he stood for."

It was an unfashionable view in his day but, in a world of changing ways, he stuck to his convictions: no movement should encourage a romantic escape from the realities of the Christian life.

CHAPTER THIRTEEN

Professor and Disciples

FROM TIME TO time Professor Rookmaaker would take a group of neophyte art students round one of Holland's art museums where he would stand them in front of a painting and open their eyes with a simple question:

"Now, what are you looking at?"

Silence. What can we say that isn't childishly obvious? "A crucifixion?" someome murmurs hesitantly, waiting to get his head cut off.

"Never mind. Begin with the obvious. But never stop with the obvious. Keep looking."

Little by little details are listed: the background landscape, the storm clouds, the Temple in the lower corner, the skull on the ground.

"Well, well, you haven't seen anything yet. No-one has yet mentioned the colours."

Colours? The group steps back and half closes its eyes. Someone grows suddenly wise, "I know, I know! It's really a Christian picture! The green is symbolic of growing things like the power of Creation and the red is the Blood of the Lamb! Wow!"

Rookmaaker quells him with a look, "Well, that is your interpretation. You are free to your opinions even though they are quite wrong. I am asking you what was in the intentions of this artist when he painted the picture. Look. And at the same time, listen. What things is he telling you about the world? And about this event in history?"

A voice at the back says something to its neighbour and Rookmaaker pounces, "Yes? Someone at the back said something about the three figures. Can you tell it please so we can all hear?"

"I'm not sure, Professor, but it's as though there are only two colours and it seems—oh, I could be wrong, sort of reading things into it . . ."

"Yes, yes, go on; I think you are beginning to arrive somewhere."

Helplessly the girl waves her hands, "It sort of binds the figures together so you think of them as one. Well, maybe it is just for composition but—no, I remember what you said last week about how composition isn't just arrangement of objects but is part of what the artist is trying to say."

By now some of the group are looking at the Professor, trying to read approval or scorn in his eyes. How are they supposed to see those colours? Others are looking at the picture and wondering for themselves if it is so.

"Do the rest of you see that, those two colours?"

Heads obediently nod.

"Or do you see something more?" Those who know him best can detect a wicked gleam in his eye.

Something more to see? Jaws obediently sag and heads tilt. The group takes another step backward and half closes its eyes again.

"Well, you are quite right; there isn't anything more. In fact, this is a silly picture. I wanted you to begin with it so you will recognise such a thing immediately and never waste your time with it again. It was painted at a time when such things had become clichés. The artist has little idea of composition of forms; see how he has been so careful to include every possible symbol of the Passion in the frame. That is why I asked you what you could see. You were all good children; you noticed all the little bits and pieces that the artist wanted you to see."

The group grins ruefully, but these people will never again be taken in by pious mid-Victoriana.

Some casual visitors to the gallery, hearing a man speaking in front of a picture, hover near the back fringes of the group. Rookmaaker immediately glares at them, "This is a special art history course. It costs two thousand dollars. Please go away."

The parasites disposed of, he flashes a smile to the back of his own group, "You were right about the colours, Sally; it is the one redeeming feature of this artist's work. If you look at his earlier paintings you will see that colour was always his strong point. Apart from that, this is a silly picture that has tried to borrow ideas from an age when the ideas were really believed. Now I will show you how this painting has its place in the historic stream, then we will go into this room behind me and see . . ."

The group trots after him. The boy who thought he was clever about Christian symbolism feels an inch high and furious. The shy girl from the back of the group is ready to die for her little Dutchman. In between those two extremes there are minds that have begun to work for themselves. Two students nudge each other, grinning. It appears that Sally is Rookmaaker's "Special Girl" this year.

"You must not think that what I tell you is the end of things," he says, taking up his stance in front of another canvas, "I have merely begun to think. Now it is for all of you to continue where I point out the way. You must take my ideas further. You must stand on my shoulders."

He continually trained them in ways to look and learn. "When you arrange to meet a friend at an art gallery, do not say, 'Meet me outside the door' but say 'Meet me in front of such and such a painting.' If by good chance your friend is late, you will learn by being with that picture for a time. You must give yourself time."

The more they learned, the more he demanded of them. One student said, "I can't forget those tedious days when Rookmaaker made us stand before one painting for a whole week. He was a tireless scholar with his motto *The more you know the more you see.* He insisted it was not the other way round."

He distinguished between students and disciples, saying that while the former merely learned from him, the latter took his ideas further. His search for disciples never stopped.

In January 1969 John Walford was talking to a friend about a seventeenth-century Dutch painting that he had bought at the Hypermarket in Kensington High Street in London. His

friend said, "You ought to meet Professor Rookmaaker."
John had never heard of him. "I'll give you his address,"
said the friend. "Why not write and ask him about the
picture?"

John wrote, enclosing photos of the painting, hoping for
nothing more than a lead as to who the artist might be, since
the small canvas was unsigned. To his surprise the return
letter announced that Rookmaaker was to be in London the
following week. They arranged to meet on Friday morning
at John's house, a four-floor pad he shared with six other
people. He was shy of meeting a Continental Professor and
planned to have the place presentable for him. But the
Professor came a day early.

"That Wednesday there had been a terrific party and the
next morning I was still under the effects of it and so was the
house. Bottles and mess on all four floors. An electrician was
due to be coming for some reason so when I heard the
doorbell at about ten a.m. I fell out of bed, put on trousers
and the first shirt I could find and went down, barefoot, to
let the electrician in."

A dapper little man stood on the doorstep. He uttered the
single word of introduction: "Rookmaaker."

It seemed an impossible situation. John had a stereogram
in his room with extensions on every floor. That morning
the Beatles were playing very loud and he could only turn
them off by going to the top of the house. But Rookmaaker
seemed quite unperturbed.

"He didn't turn a hair at the mess. Was just interested in
talking about art and looking at the picture. I know now that
it was the informality of the meeting that suited him. He is a
very shy man and very awkward with initial contacts. It
suited me too."

That spring, John went to his parents' house in Hamp-
shire to spend his holiday studying the Bible. "The first day I
prayed to be guided towards a theme. What God led me to
started in Deuteronomy. As the week went on I made
written notes." He discovered a theme of God's hand in
history, the way God's blessing or curse works its way out
through the whole fabric of existence; crops and herds,

135

physical health, peace with other nations.

Towards September, Rookmaaker wrote telling John he should come to a conference at Ashburnham where he was speaking. John was not interested.

"I was so sick of Christian conferences. I was sick of hearing the same old thing every time. I'd had some conflict with some of my fellow Christians because I thought they had reduced Christianity to a kind of sausage machine for making more Christians. Conversion wasn't a renewal of the quality of life to them; it was only changing your status. Also there were some of them who thought all the works of art I had were a kind of idolatry and that I should sell them all and give the money to the poor."

But a week before the conference, John decided to go. He described it as a staggering experience. "The talk Rookmaaker gave was on God's hand in history, starting in Deuteronomy. He could have been giving that talk from the notes I had been making during my spring holiday. It was an enrichment and elaboration of what I had come to when I spent that week aside with the Lord, but it was the same thing. What Rookmaaker said made absolute sense. He was on the same wavelength as myself but twenty years further on in study and reflection. To him, Christianity was relevant to every area of life; it could renew the whole fabric."

In October, Rookmaaker was in England again for three days, bringing a group of his students to look at English country houses: Hampton Court, Sion House and Strawberry Hill. He asked John to drive their minicab. He noticed the Englishman's verbal reaction to paintings, landscape gardening and architecture. After the trip he took him out to dinner at an Italian restaurant, noisy and rather dark. Graham joined them at the last minute.

"John," said the Professor, "you have a very good eye; you have a pronounced flair in your reaction to works of art. But you have absolutely no sense of historical perspective. You say you plan to teach English at a small public school?" He rolled out one of his favourite English words, "That is crraizy—*crraizy*! You ought to come and study art history with me."

"But the language—"

"Pooh! That is nothing. You can sit at the back of my lectures and pick up Dutch as you go."

"I'm not sure. Surely it makes more sense to study art history in England where I can do it in my own language?"

At that point Graham put a crucial question: "If you were going to study theology, would you want to study with an atheist? Or would you think you could learn more by studying from someone who believed the Bible?"

John gave him the obvious answer.

"Frankly," said Graham, "it's no different studying art history. I think you will find if you go to the—" [he mentioned a well-known art centre in London] "that their method of teaching art history is as much based on their humanist or Marxist beliefs as a method of teaching theology is based on the beliefs of that teacher."

John made his decision on the spot, sewed up the loose ends of his affairs in England and a fortnight later was in Holland.

Rookmaaker's suggestion for learning the language was unworkable. "It was a bit of a problem," said John, with classic British understatement. It was the winter of 1969, and the language labs were filled with Czech refugees. John had a heartbreaking experience of struggling with Dutch grammar; he described the first year in Holland as the hardest year he had ever spent. The answer to his prayer for help came in the shape of Hans van Seventer who sat at the back of the lecture hall and gave a running translation of Rookmaaker's words in English. Even so, the curriculum was daunting; it included philosophy, archaeology and medieval Latin, all taught in Dutch. John slogged on among the community of Christian scholars, developing his ideas through contact with his chosen teacher.

After a while he found his own tendency to romanticism was being curbed as he acquired a more Christian mind. Rookmaaker loved the work of the Golden Age painter, van Goyen, because he was an artist who delighted in the character of the world as it is, with all its brokenness and shortcomings. Van Goyen did not paint idealised, dream-

137

like landscapes but the real world, making it enjoyable on its own terms.

"Compare van Goyen," said Rookmaaker, "with the work of Claude or any of the Italianate painters. They present a world you can never have. It is good to have dreams but if the quality of that dream is forced it will only lead to frustration. We must dream towards an attainable end."

One day the students were outside a Dutch country house after a lecture. The sun blazed and the birds were singing. John said impulsively to a friend, "What a lovely day. It's a pity we haven't got a swimming pool here."

Rookmaaker butted in with anger. "If you think like that you will never enjoy life! You will always be frustrated and you will never make the most of opportunities around you! There is so much to enjoy. If you think only of what isn't there, you'll never be happy!"

During one of his trips to England, Rookmaaker visited John's parents in their Georgian house, to sip Pimms No. One on the terrace where the grandmother sat beneath an old-fashioned sunshade. The setting delighted him and his host and hostess' graciousness stirred early memories. Things had not been easy in the Marxist orientated student world but his childhood atmosphere of sunlight on white marble was alive and well and living in England.

Later, when his new disciple announced his engagement to an Italian art student, the Professor wrote reassuringly to his parents, using the one argument that would be bound to appeal to English gentry. "When gentlemen of the eighteenth-century went to Europe on their Grand Tour, there were certainly some who returned home with Italian wives. So, after all, your son has done what is very traditional."

It was John and Maria, living in their cottage outside Amsterdam, who began the tradition of having the Professor stay overnight after the late Wednesday seminar. He enjoyed a nightcap of Marsala, and conversations lasting till three a.m. were not unusual. He always asked to be woken at seven a.m., reappearing ten minutes later, spruce and shaved and ready to continue his deep discussion over tea and a lightly-stirred fried egg. Not a minute was wasted in casual talk.

The cottage was tiny and the guest bedroom was up a rickety ladder in the attic. The prospect of their beloved Professor crashing through the ladder in the middle of the night was so appalling that John spent the afternoon of his first visit re-nailing every rung.

One day one of Rookmaaker's pretty art students told him she would like to marry an academic. "Just like you, Professor."

"Well, Winnie, let me tell you what it is like to be the wife of such a man. You see your husband for breakfast but you dare not speak for fear of deranging his thoughts. Er . . . do you say that in English? Deranging? Yes. Well, you do not speak for fear that he becomes deranged. Then you may see him at supper but not for the rest of the evening because he is at his desk. And remember that a serious academic does not go to bed at a normal time." He twinkled at her. "You want to live like that? You would wilt."

Winnie was one of his Special Girls. It was said that Rookmaaker understood the problems a pretty girl has to face when she wants her ideas to be taken seriously. A more worldly explanation is that he enjoyed being surrounded by attractive young women who hung on his every word. He basked in the company of admiring art students, especially if they were soft girls with butterfly eyes. He beamed approvingly at the well rounded ones. "Eat up that second piece of cake; we want you to look like Hendrickje Stöffels." (Rembrandt's well-upholstered common-law wife.) He could look a fully dressed student over skilfully. "I know exactly how Rubens would have painted you." But there was enough of Christ in the man to make the girls feel safe in his presence.

Living in the closeknit, gossipy world of a university, he dared to single out one pretty girl, spending extra time with her questions in the lecture hall. Soon she became known among the students as Rooky's Special. There was a different Special every year.

But in spite of the nudges and winks that surrounded him, no scent of scandal ever stuck to his name. He took his marriage vows seriously, returning home in the evenings to a well-ordered house, a well-prepared meal and all the comfortable *gazelligheid* of his native land. Anky gave him the love and continuity that his childhood had lacked. Because of it, he had security to pursue his studies, for his true love was Wisdom.

> I esteemed her more than sceptres and thrones;
> compared with her, I held riches as nothing.
> I reckoned no priceless stone to be her peer,
> for compared with her, all gold is a pinch of sand,
> and beside her silver ranks as mud.
> I loved her more than health and beauty,
> preferred her to the light,
> since her radiance never sleeps.
> In her company all good things came to me,
> at her hands riches not to be numbered.
> Book of Wisdom 7: 8–11

One day at the VU, Winnie complained that she was tired of going over the same arguments about the reliability of Scripture. "It just seems like we never get beyond it, Professor. As soon as someone begins to take the Bible seriously, you meet some other guy who comes along and knocks it all down again. There's so much more to talk about. I'm tired of fighting for the Bible."

Rookmaaker rounded on her, his eyes beady and cold, "You are tired! I am sorry for you! I am not tired yet. I have fought for the Bible for most of my life. As for those people there"—he jerked the stem of his pipe towards the part of the VU where the theological faculty did their work—"they are tired of it too. Some of them think I am a museum piece because I still talk about the historical resurrection of Christ and all the great supernatural events of this real world."

"But I only said—" The girl's eyes filled with tears.

"Yes, 'only'. And now you are weeping! Never mind. Weep for the right things. Weep because the truth of God is being thrown away and what will our world do without it?

140

Men will find other moral standards that they build society on, never doubt that. Did I ever tell you what I saw in the war? You cannot imagine what it is like when men turn away from God. The thought should make you go cold.

"It begins here. It begins when people say, 'I can forget what the Bible tells me and I can let it slide away from history.' It begins when men say that the righteous God does no longer work in history. Or that He never did. Or that He never could because He never was there." Rook-maaker looked at the girl's unlined face and honey-coloured hair. "I have fought for the truth of the Bible for thirty years. But are you tired already? How can you be? How do you dare!"

CHAPTER FOURTEEN

The Flying Dutchman

THE STUDENT WORLD of the 1960s was very different from the world of Hans Rookmaaker's youth. Rock music hammered down hard on old standards; John, George, Paul and Ringo put Merseyside on the map. Grass was something more interesting than the stuff Dad mowed on Sunday afternoons. The Pill was easy to come by and so were some of the girls. Caught off guard, some Christians continued to fight out-of-date battles, like Don Quixote tilting at windmills in an age when tilting and jousting had been ousted by gunpowder. Christian Art meant designing a cover for a tract and even that was slightly suspect. Meanwhile, out in the real world, the Spontaneous Generation had traded their Christian birthright for a message of pot.

A Travelling Secretary for Inter-Varsity Fellowship described the situation in British Arts Colleges: "Anyone who was a convinced Christian and who was studying art usually opted out during Pre-Dip and went into missionary work or else went completely secular and relegated their Christianity to Sunday mornings. They had given up the struggle and retreated into pietism. There wasn't anyone I could see who was trying to bring Christianity and art together. It was a case of living with a split mind."

One day in September 1967 an IVF Travelling Secretary was called into her employer's office. "A graphics designer has invited a Professor Hans Rookmaaker over to speak at the Birmingham College of Art," Oliver Barclay told her.

"Invited who?"

"Rookmaaker. He's Dutch. He's got a very pronounced point of view." Barclay outlined what he saw as the main points of Dooyeweerdianism, adding, "So don't be over-influenced by his type of thinking. Just see if he could be helpful. He's arriving at Euston. Escort him to the College, Meryl, and let me know how it turns out. Your predecessor knew about him, by the way; she used to say he looked like Harold Wilson."

At the appointed time Meryl Fergus made her way through the Euston crowds. A man was standing by the ticket barrier with a small suitcase at his feet. He was a neatly dressed, professorial type with a grey scarf knotted depressingly under his chin. They shook hands. To Meryl the little man looked quite dead. She wondered how he was going to be received in a potentially hostile college.

She steered the foreigner to the ticket window and got out her purse. "Two returns to Birmingham, please." A slightly accented voice behind her said, "First Class." It was a voice accustomed to being obeyed.

"First? Oh, er yes, of course." Meryl did a rapid calculation through the contents of her purse and thought, *I only hope he's worth it*. They sat in the immaculate emptiness of the First Class carriage. Conversation was stilted but there was everything to find out about the strange little man.

Finally the train pulled into Birmingham station where a group of students hovered near the ticket barrier. There were introductions all round, then an awkward pause. The little man seemed so foreign and so formal. Small talk sagged and died. Oh dear, how good was his command of English? One young man had a flash of inspiration. "Like something to eat before the meeting, er . . . sir?"

Yes, he would very much. Thank you.

They took the Son of the Resident to a student café near the College, sat him on a stool at the counter and fed him on eggs and bangers. He was polite but small talk did not work.

Back at the College the Christian Union people had done their publicity well; seventy students were waiting to hear the lecture "Three Steps to Modern Art". The name Rookmaaker was known in the arts-school world because of his published thesis, so they were ready to take him seriously.

While he was being formally introduced Meryl found herself wishing she was anywhere but there. Writers did not always make good speakers, neither did foreigners. Besides, what if he pushed Dooyeweerdianism too far? She had seen too many platform speakers verbally savaged by students to feel at ease that evening. Dooyeweerd or no Dooyeweerd, she would hate to see the Professor put down after travelling so far.

Hans Rookmaaker surveyed the hairy audience, stepped to the podium and came alive. "Why do you call it 'modern' art? It has been around for seventy years." He developed his theme, showing slides. He knew his subject inside out. He held the students' attention in the palm of his hand.

Some belligerent questions shot back towards the podium and Rookmaaker fielded them with ease, like a man used to handling controversy. He seemed to be using the audience's mind to continue his lecture, as though he and they were active participants in a mutual process of learning. His status of Professor gave him credence in the College. His Christian beliefs were unashamed. Wondering how she could describe the evening to her employer, Meryl realised there was something more here than Christian beliefs tacked onto an academic discipline. Here was a Christian mind.

The Professor's eyes ranged over the audience, "You have more questions? No? Well, afterwards I will stay and we can talk more. No-one has asked me about the hard-edge style that is coming out of America, about Oldenburg or Warhol. I had thought you would like to talk about that. But later, maybe."

That was different too. Most lecturers collected their fee and were only too glad to get home to their wives and children. Rookmaaker was more like an undergraduate.

"Come now, you will not all go to bed yet, I am sure. The night is young. Shall we go and drink—oh no, the pubs are closed. Meryl, you know where we can find coffee?"

A group collected itself from the audience, took the Professor to another café and stayed there till it closed, hunched over their coffee cups, their eyes on the little man who seemed so relaxed among them. They asked questions they had barely begun to formulate. They were flippant, then fierce, and finally frank. They asked things they had pushed aside in the moments when an atheistic world-view had seemed too pervasive to fight any more. Rookmaaker listened. He answered the questions behind the questions. Most of all, he spoke as a man speaks who has been down into darkness and thought his own way towards the light. In subsequent years he would refer to the Birmingham group as his most favourite children who best put his ideas into practice.

At closing time they delivered him safe and sound to sleep in the spare room of somebody's Mum's house. The next day, September 26th, Meryl was to escort him back to London to lecture at the National Club.

The setting could not have been in greater contrast. The National was in the Army and Navy Club in Piccadilly; a clubland of leather armchairs, tall windows and Jeeves. The lecture had been discreetly advertised as "The Cultural Situation, a Spectacle of Protest". The printed invitations, R.S.V.P., were in copperplate script and the cards were edged in gold. Dhr. Braaksma, the Cultural Attaché of the Dutch Embassy, was there with Sir Arthur Smith and notables from the Tate. "Professor Rookmaaker? *Delighted* to meet you. *So* glad you could come. Oh, *may* I introduce . . ."

But with Rookmaaker around, things did not go as expected, as David Hanson, the organiser, remembered:

"Hans had taken a couple of tickets with him with a strict warning as to their distribution. On the 26th, from about half past six in the evening, a variety of artists and art students in beards, jeans and plimsolls, began to converge on the National Club and by eight p.m. we had an audience of considerably more than had been expected and of a very different constitution!

"Throughout the lecture, with its recorded illustrations by the Beatles and others, we had the faces of somewhat perplexed retired Admirals, Generals and other officers, poked around the door to find out what on earth was going on in their dining room. Many of them lived in the Club in retirement. The lecture was a great success, but I was 'carpeted' by the Club steward the following day."

Rookmaaker tailored his words to fit his Club audience. When he mentioned pop groups like the Grateful Dead or Jefferson Airplane, he took a moment to explain who they were. From time to time he flicked on the tape recorder to illustrate his points with contemporary music. The room was washed by the flat, nasal voice of Bob Dylan: "Something is happening here but you don't know what it is, do you, Mr. Jones?"

Meryl watched the faces of the elegant gentlemen: "You could see the light slowly dawning. To begin with they'd been sitting back with expressions of 'oh-fascinating-do-tell-me-more'. By the time he'd finished, they had listened to young generation music for the first time. They were shaken and serious."

Reactions were, "I didn't know this was happening. I mean, I never listened before." "My children have this music playing all day long but I never thought about what it was saying." "But what should we do?"

He was merciless. "You took Christian standards for granted. The young people said to you, 'Why do life like this or that way?' and you said, 'Never bother me with questions; just do it.' But they are intelligent young men and women. They have looked at the world and they have made up their own standards. You say we should fight pornography? Yes, we should fight pornography, but remember it only came this far because we Christians were not there when we should have been there. Now the battle is lost and we can only clean up the battlefield. So do not say 'Wicked young people sleeping with each other,' but say 'Wicked Christians who did not explain well when the questions were being asked.' What questions are being asked today? That is for you to find out."

He advised them to re-evaluate their own position in the light of Scripture; to listen and look and read what the young generation was producing. He told them never to apologise for the truth.

Next day Meryl was back in Oliver Barclay's office. She described what she had seen in Birmingham and at the National, ending, "There's no-one else talking this way from a Christian base. There are so many places we can use him!"

The best solution was to bring the students to the Professor, so a conference was arranged for a summer weekend in 1968. Meryl looked out of the conference house window on Friday afternoon. Bearded young men in denims and girls in long skirts were climbing out of disreputable cars and ambling up the driveway. Many of them were carrying canvasses. They spread their work along the inside walls and waited for the Professor to make comments.

Rookmaaker ambled up and down, pointing at one or other picture with his toe, "Yes, yes," he drawled, sounding bored, "quite nice . . . that has something . . ."

An artist dared to draw his attention to a painting, "This is the one I've been working on since last year."

"Yes? Well, I have seen your work already in Holland. I think it is all right."

"Do you think I'm on the right track?" A year's agonising had gone into the question.

"Well, it's nice, what you do." He wandered away.

Students learned the hard way. Rookmaaker would not evaluate a picture till he had lived with it for a while, preferably a lifetime. His strength was in making people think. Soon he was holding forth to a small group. "A Christian artist, what is that? A man who paints a cover for a religious book or designs the glass window of a church? Maybe he does these things, but a Christian artist is someone who looks at reality in a deeper way than others." He gestured to the collage of a nude and, for once, committed himself with a comment, "You see that? What does the artist say to us about Woman? That she is beautiful, a creature made by God? Look at it and listen to what it is telling you. There are many such pictures nowadays in art galleries and street posters and you know what they say about Woman: that she is ugly, obscene, a piece of machinery for prostitution. A woman like this is not to be a companion or a friend; she is not to love but only to—" He said a word that had never before been said in a Christian conference.

On the fringes of the group the young artist responsible for the picture wished the floor would swallow him up. "But we must not think this artist really feels this about Woman," continued Rookmaaker, knowing full well the artist would be somewhere within earshot, "He is a Christian, that is why he is here. He must learn how to look at Woman and think how to portray her. Not as the world teaches him to look at her but as God and His Word teaches him to look at her."

"You mean romantically?"

The word was a red rag to a bull, "No, no! Not with romance! We do not deal with romance! We are Christians; the true realists of this world!"

That Arts weekend was the first of many. Evangelicals who were interested in the arts appeared as if from nowhere and conference speakers began to include poets and film-makers, radio men, designers and architects. Rookmaaker was untiring on the IVF circuit.

"He practically killed several Travelling Secretaries," Meryl remembered, "He'd stay up talking half the night and still expect you to be around to carry his suitcase next morning!"

He demanded much of himself too; when American Christians discovered him, journeys of several hundred miles a week were not uncommon. In spite of the work load he delighted to collect new experiences. There was a little spare time during one English trip so Meryl and Tony Wales, her successor in the job, invited the Professor to walk on Hampstead Heath. They ended at the fairground where Tony explained the sport of Dodgem cars.

"Yes, yes, I can see for myself. You hit each other with little cars. Well, go ahead. Meryl and I will wait for you here." He leaned over the guard rail and prepared to watch.

A few minutes later the Travelling Secretary climbed out of his car and turned to leave, when the Professor announced, "Now I too will do this."

"You, Professor? Er, you do know it can get a bit rough out there?"

"Yes, yes, I know, I can see. Come on, Meryl." Tony took his second ride and for the next five minutes they thumped each other around while music blared and overhead sparks crackled and flashed. Finally the Professor of Art History clambered out of the car and shook himself back into shape. "You take away all my dignity."

He could remove other people's dignity very efficiently. Some young men at one British Arts Conference were too uncritical, so he decided to have a little fun at their expense. Lecturing continuously about architecture, he led them to the Gents. They trooped after him, taking notes. Rookmaaker gave them a whirlwind tour of the facilities, ad libbing about the philosophy that lay behind the lines of the plumbing. On another occasion, when minimal-art was in vogue, he treated one of his friends to a straight-faced discourse on the position of three chairs and the shape of the space between them.

"Now tell me about the Christian Union." Rookmaaker was in Oxford in the early 1970s. He was having supper at a Chinese restaurant before speaking at the C.U. meeting. The colonial-born Professor handled chop-sticks like a native. The C.U. President spoke warmly about the opportunities for evangelism and guiding a new believer's devotional life.

"But what is your area of study?"

"Oh that. I'm reading economics, actually. When I'm not being C.U. President, that is."

Rookmaaker glanced up, steely-eyed and dropped a small bombshell into the chow mein. "How much thinking have you done from a Biblical base in relation to your work?"

"How much—er, I don't quite see."

"How have you applied your Christian faith to your economics?"

A student from Uganda remembers the effect of Rookmaaker's teaching at that period of his life: "The challenge I got from Rookmaaker was a constant attempt to relate my

Christian faith to my academic career. As a matter of fact, Rookmaaker taught that the academic career is the outcome of one's Christian faith and not the other way round."

That evening in Oxford he spoke to Evangelical students about Christian principles in art, tracing the breakdown of standards from Ensor to the present day. Someone raised a hand to ask about evangelism and a moment later the evening passed the point of no return.

"Why should you spend your life evangelising?" asked Rookmaaker. "There are more important things to do in the world."

A horrified wriggle swept through the audience. What about John 3:16? What about the command to do the work of an evangelist? Shock was expressed with Oxbridgian decorum. Was he really suggesting they should scrap The Great Commission? "Surely, Dr. Rookmaaker, in the light of Romans 10:14 you cannot be serious?" "Really, I would have thought—" Favourite Bible verses began to thicken the air between audience and speaker.

Rookmaaker waved them aside like so many flies. "I have done twenty-five years thinking, relating Biblical principles to art. You should be willing to do the same in your areas of life and work."

As he drove the Professor back to his flat in London later that night, Tony said, "That remark of yours really put the cat among the pigeons."

Rookmaaker puffed contentedly, filling the car with smoke. "They will survive."

But evangelism happened in his ministry. Tony recalled, "I know of people who came to faith in Christ through the lecture 'Three Steps to Modern Art' in which John 3:16 appeared nowhere. And I was at a London Art School when Rooky gave his 'Beat, Rock, Protest' lecture. At the end, the head of the painting department said, 'Now, for the first time, I understand my son.' "

Tony and the Professor arrived at the tiny flat as midnight passed. Rooky was ready to stay up and talk. Fortunately Tony and his flatmate were ready for the same thing. In the small hours Hans retired to the bedroom while the other two

150

unrolled their sleeping bags on the living room floor. Jokingly, Tony called to their distinguished guest, "Like to bring us early morning tea?"

Sleep held them all till far past breakfast time. At ten a.m. the two younger men opened their eyes to see a stout figure in a dressing gown. An unlit pipe was clamped between his teeth. Clunk. He put a tray of tea on the floor beside them. "Early morning tea, indeed! This is why the British nation is going to the dogs!"

But he was a confirmed Anglophile and he kept in touch with his friends there. On one occasion in 1974, after he had stayed with an IVF friend and his wife, he left a thank-you present of a Duke Ellington album inscribed, "In order that you may hear more as you know more." It was a reference to their discussion of epistemology the night before.

He discovered an IVF Staff Member's mutual fondness for Glenfiddich malt whisky and by small, well-timed gifts when he visited England, he kept Tim Dean in Glenfiddich for years. Travelling by train with Tony he admired English scenery, saying that landscape gardening was the only true English art form.

On one of those long train journeys Tony casually mentioned the TV programme *Candid Camera*. The name was not familiar so he described it to Rookmaaker.

"Yes, yes! We have this also in Holland! I remember one programme when—" He launched into a blow-by-blow description of a series of Dutch practical jokes. Tony had the impression they would be described as schoolboy humour. Rookmaaker's accent became more and more incomprehensible. Tears of mirth spilled from his eyes. He roared, he gasped for breath, he babbled, he spluttered, he groaned, he rocked in his seat. Finally he subsided to a point near exhaustion and for the next few miles only an occasional giggle broke the silence. Tony gathered that the humour, whatever it was, had reached something very basic in Hans Rookmaaker.

On one London trip, Rooky and his friends went to Schmidt's German Restaurant. They filled one long table and waiters pushed another to join it. Menus were handed round. "Oh, this is going to take ages." "Let's see, can we divide into fours or something?" "How many of us, thirty?" Waiters hovered along the tableful, ready for orders.

A Dutch voice rose from one end, "This is going to take far too long and we all want to talk about even more important things than food." He clicked his fingers at the nearest waiter. "Thirty wiener schnitzels and thirty coffees. Thank you. Now, Jeff, you asked about the Mannerists. If you had been listening to my talk this morning you should have known where they came from. I did not spell it out. Maybe I should have. But tell me your interest in them and we can go on from where you are in your thinking now." The student hooked his hair behind his ears, planted both elbows on the table and began to argue his point.

From the 1970s, the back pages of Hans Rookmaaker's appointment diaries list more names and addresses in the U.K. and U.S. than in the Netherlands. For the next seven years he zigzagged across the Atlantic, the only person anyone knew in those days who could talk intelligently about Christianity and the arts. The place-names in the diaries read like the itinerary of a politician's whistle-stop tour: Birmingham, Vancouver, Chicago, London, Seattle, San Francisco, Bristol, Edinburgh, Denver, Chattanooga, Toronto.

His book *Modern Art and the Death of a Culture* was published in 1970, reaching a wider readership than his thesis. Malcolm Muggeridge made it his *Observer* Book of the year for 1972. A British friend tried to arrange for the two men to meet, but they were both so busy it proved impossible.

Rookmaaker had close American friends but he never fully adapted to the New World way of doing things and his failure puzzled him. He was used to the debating style of the feint and parry of Old World swordsmanship. The direct shootout of the cowboy West was not to his liking. He refused to give packaged answers, once telling a girl, "I am the Pope of Christian Art History. I have the answers to your questions right here in my pocket and I am not telling you. Think for yourself!"

But his knowledge of art was not exhaustive. He once dismissed a group of Louis le Blond prints as "of no value". His Calvinism coloured everything. He described the Mass as "only theatre"—a strangely belittling use of the word from a man who stood head and shoulders above contemporary Evangelicals in seeing the value of all the arts.

During a conference at Lookout Mountain, Tennessee, he decided to miss Francis Schaeffer's Saturday evening lecture in favour of a visit to the Grand Ole Opry, a Country and Western show in Nashville. To that end he harried one of his friends all week. "Now, Carl, you do remember that on Saturday evening you are driving me to the Grand Ole Opry."

"But, Professor, I had wanted to hear—"

"No, Carl. Saturday is the last time the Grand Ole Opry is playing at their original premises and you are to take me there. Now remember." He got his way.

He persevered on the lecture circuit and whenever he found kindred spirits the joy was mutual and lasting. Others thought of him as a funny little Dutchman who smoked all the time and showed nude pictures. Said one editor, "Undoubtedly he was a great man, but what feet of clay!"

When he visited Wheaton Christian College, he was asked what he thought of the Chapel on campus. The Dutchman gave his opinion without equivocation. He looked over the highly-thought-of chapel interior, picked out in gold and white, then asked how Christians could worship Christ in a building that was designed to look like a Greek temple.

By the mid-seventies there were signs of an increasing dogmatism; the pressure of teaching had begun to take its toll. Rookmaaker had become the star speaker at Evangelical arts conferences, events that would have been unthinkable when he began his ministry. In the enormous U.S. he suffered from the inevitable weakness of the conference system. Travel took a disproportionate amount of time compared with that spent with individuals. The star speaker was not allowed to develop friendships with artists who wanted to take his ideas further. There was no time. He felt he was pouring his words through a sieve and only the most superficial statements were sinking into his audience's mind.

He would return to Europe after those trips exhausted and depressed. He had poured out everything he knew like a man trying to educate his lover to greater joys. His audience smiled a bright smile, shrugged her shoulders and turned to the next man. "Yes, all very interesting, Herr Professor, but how can art best be used for evangelism?"

Rookmaaker confided his frustration to a British IVF Staff Member. "Out of a thousand who hear me speak, maybe twelve take in what I am saying, and no more than five begin to put things into practice. The others—pooh!—they listen to a nice speaker. They say, 'Yes I heard him lecture on . . . what was it, now? But it was *so* enjoyable! Ah yes, it was about how moral standards in our society are breaking down. I *did* enjoy his talk!' Then they forget."

After one lecture the Professor bowed his grey head onto the podium and began to pray. "Father, we thank you for the possibilities you gave us to think, that you put us into this world and gave us consciousness; that you told us who you are. We thank you that you are on the great golden throne and that you have your Son with you, sitting on your right hand side, governing this world. And that what we do therefore has meaning and that we can work in this world.

"It is promised that you will be with us and that the great bits of history—we can accept them out of your hands. Forgive us that we went out of this world and left the wounded by the side of the road, not to touch with our hands the unpious, the unholy.

"Thank you that you gave us the brains that we can think. Thank you that you gave us compassion that we can feel with the others. Thank you that you called us to be your children. Thank you, in Jesus' name."

In July 1976 Jan, Graham, Hans and JoAnn decided to have an art evening of their own in Jan's home in Zwigglete. Rookmaaker heard about the plan and turned up. It wasn't that he didn't trust his spiritual children to do things on their own. He was like a father who had not been invited to the baptism. They welcomed him and he listened politely for most of the evening. When there was a pause, he said, "Graham, may I say something now?"

"Of course, of course."

Jan, a tall man, had been leaning against the dining table. He moved from his place. The Professor backed up to the table and there was a brief struggle as he tried to hitch his broad bottom over the edge. Finally he succeeded and sat with his feet dangling above the floor.

Rookmaaker had seldom spoken of his own life, though he once mentioned to Graham that such-and-such a thing should be mentioned "when someone writes my biography". What the friends at Zwigglete heard that evening was the closest anyone had heard to a Rookmaaker autobiography.

"Many years ago during the war years, I became a Christian. I was interested in what was happening in the world then and to the Jews. I read the Bible looking for answers and I became a Christian. When I came into the church, to my great amazement I noticed two things: there was a tremendous lack of freedom and there was absolutely no interest in art.

"I was puzzled by the lack of freedom because freedom is so important in the Bible. We have freedom from the past; we don't have to do what Christians in the past did just *because* they did it, but only if it seems good to us now. We can learn from them but not be bound by them.

"We have freedom from the future; we don't have to make things for our grandchildren but to work in this world now. We have freedom from today; we don't have to be *modieuse* [trendy]. We must have this freedom if we don't want to be prostitutes to our own time.

"The second problem I found was the negative attitude towards art. Though I met it in Reformed Evangelical circles, it is not only in those circles. In the past I have talked negatively about this but lately I ask more positive questions and I feel now that is the best way. Just work with art and let people see what you do.

"In the fifties I felt Christians should begin to work with art but where should we begin? There is hardly any tradition to build on. You can know the writer of a book is a Christian by the way he writes, but in painting or music or graphics? It is hard to find any work that speaks of Christ. So we must begin to think together how it can be done.

"I give you two reasons to make a work of art: that you love God and that you love your neighbour. Remember where the problems of your own age of history lie. Then go to work.

"Dare to be yourself and dare to be an individual. Defend your freedom *hant en tant* [tooth and nail]. There is now no tradition to build on. We need to begin anew. Maybe something will come out of it if we are busy. Maybe we'll all be in concentration camps ten years from now, but that's not the point. We have responsibility only for today: to love God and our neighbour and to live honest and straight lives.

"As for me, I want to think of history. Society changes, but what lies behind the changes? That is what we must always ask. We know that what a man believes makes him live a certain way. If he believes nothing of the truth, that too makes him live a certain way. So when we look at history it is not only politics and economics. We must demand spiritual explanations too and spiritual solutions. What we do has results in God's world and what we do not do, also. You and I are not caught in the mesh of history as the technocrats and behaviourists are caught. As Christians we can have a great certainty that God eventually wins." Before JoAnn clicked off the tape recorder, Rookmaaker spoke of his own future.

"The art historians never talk about Calvin or the Reformation and what it all meant. I hope to be thinking about these things in the coming years."

In January 1977 he spoke at a church in suburban London, outlining a view of reality that took in more than material things. Afterwards a journalist, who should have known better, said, "You are looking tired, Dr. Rookmaaker." He backed away from the personal remark as if he had been flicked with a whip. "No, no, no. I am all right, I am all right. I am not tired."

But he was. He seemed to have shrunk, like a figure seen through the wrong end of a telescope. The lecture was as interesting as ever. The man had grown grey and weary. He spent the night at Tony Wales' flat before flying back to his new home near the *Kortenhoeve* community in Gelderland.

CHAPTER FIFTEEN

The Teacher of *Kortenhoeve*

THE ROOKMAAKERS HAD originally thought of buying a house near Amsterdam for a community centre, but house prices in the west were too high so they searched further afield. The place they bought was in Eck-en-Weil, a village named for an ancient breach in a *dijk*, where silt flowed through to make good pasture.

Eck-en-Wiel is in Gelderland Province, in that great triangular base of the Netherlands that lies between the dune strip on the west, where they grow tulips, and the reclaimed peatbog in the north-east, where they grow cows. There are more trees in Gelderland than in the west or north; hedges and pollarded willows outline the fields, brushing shadows onto the grass. The landscape looks familiar to English eyes. Rembrandt was there in the late 1640s. His pictures show a friendly countryside with rising ground and trees growing from a pale, sandy soil. None of the ground rises very much and the sand is a constant reminder that this is delta land.

The village is on a boundary line in Low Countries history. The nearby Rijn, with its branches, was a natural stopping place for the Roman soldiers, becoming a face-saving line of demarcation between their civilisation and the untameable lands of the north. The same rivers were a problem to the Duke of Palma when he tried to win back the Provinces to Spanish rule. He sent his troops in up-river and from the east, re-establishing Spanish-Catholic authority as far as Gelderland. When the army dodged back to fight in France, the river became the boundary of Calvinist independence.

At the end of World War II the Allies liberated the Netherlands from the south as far up as the river where the attack at Arnhem failed, leaving the north Netherlands in Nazi hands for a further eight terrible months. The house that became the L'Abri community stood on that historic boundary line. Whatever blood was spilt on the surrounding fields was spilt a long time ago.

In the 1970s the countryside around the village was patchworked into small acreages of apple and pear trees, with floppy-eared pigs rootling in the shade, and raspberry bushes mulched down under silver-gold straw. Gelderland was the fruit farm of the Netherlands. This was the landscape of Rookmaaker's last years as a teacher.

Kortenhoeve was a great white cube of a farmhouse, built in the eighteenth century when the nation was aping the French, and Hendrik of Arnhem was courting Cornelia of Apeldoorn. The house wore a periwig of slate and curlicued attic gables. Its high windows were screened in Dutch fashion with a deep net frill across the top and a row of potted plants along the sill. It stood in splendid isolation surrounded by an orchard. That orchard was once a bone of contention.

"No, we cannot afford the extra land!" Anky insisted before the sale went through, "The Lord has given us the money for the house. We are tempting Him if we do not be content with what we have. You should not make debts, that is what the Bible says!"

Land or no land, they needed to buy the house. For years the Rookmaakers and a committee of church people had been praying for money to buy a house in the Netherlands. They had watched the crowds going to Diemen. There was obviously a need for a Christian cultural study centre and residential community. Hans and Anky sent people to Switzerland if they felt the experience would help them, but the community there had become larger. Some Dutch people returned saying they had benefited, while others were not sure; one young man came home saying he had hated it. The signs were pointing towards a small community in the Netherlands. The passing thought became a tentative prayer, then a more positive prayer and a plan. Finally the gifts of money and interest-free loans had accumulated till there was enough to buy *Kortenhoeve* and a barn to convert into a chapel, but no extra land. Husband and wife were at loggerheads.

"We need the extra land," said Hans, "We cannot have a Christian community next door to something like a caravan park. Who knows what may be put up on that land if it is not ours? No, we must continue to pray. The Lord has given us much; let us ask for more!"

Two opposing prayers rose to heaven: from Anky, that there be thankfulness for what was already given; from Hans, that more be given. As things turned out, one of his students had inherited some money and he decided it was right to invest it in the land.

The *Kortenhoeve* plot was shaped like a three-cornered hat, planted with enough apple trees to yield ten thousand kilos of fruit and separated from the road by a channel of water and bulrushes. Through a line of poplar trees beside the barn the gates of the village cemetery were just visible beyond the road.

The first Workers moved into the house on a rainy Thursday, March 18th 1973. Students arrived to listen to recorded lectures on art, culture and the Bible; to help dig the garden and wash the windows. Unmarried boy students unrolled their sleeping bags in one of the large bedrooms; the girl students settled into the other. The Workers drew up a rota of kitchen and cleaning duties and got to know the problems and needs of each guest. News of the venture spread by word of mouth and Reformed churchmen watched with interest. The Rookmaakers' methods of prayer seemed a little strange but their doctrinal teaching appeared to be soundly Calvinist and there was no doubt that Professor Rookmaaker had a way of talking to young people.

Soon after *Kortenhoeve* was bought, there were signs that all was not well with Hans' heart. There had been bouts of sleeplessness and giddy spells. John Walford spoke to him, man to man, telling him he must review his priorities. The Professor agreed, but did nothing to alter the pace of his life.

He continued at the VU and drove from Diemen to Gelderland twice a week; once to talk things over with the young community Workers and once to lead a Saturday night discussion for all the guests. Eventually he was to spend most of his weekends at the community, driving back from the VU for supper on Friday evening. From the first he pre-empted the most comfortable chair in the living room and infuriated the permanent staff with his high-handedness.

One of the Workers remembered, "We'd been laying water pipes and wiring the bedrooms for electricity all week (which was work he couldn't see). We'd been talking to spiritually interested or troubled people far into the night (which was more work he couldn't see). You know the thing he kept on harping about in the Worker's Prayer Meeting?"

Rookmaaker cleared his throat with grim meaning, "There is still no doorknob on the landing toilet. I mentioned it last week and it has not been done. Why has it not been done?"

"We've been pretty busy, Professor. Those water pipes had to be laid down before we could—"

"But I told you about this last week! It is a little thing but it must be done. When are we going to have that doorknob on the landing toilet?"

Mending doors, hanging pictures and putting up saucepan racks were all simple jobs he found pleasure in at his own home. Laying water pipes through gravelly sand in the pouring March rain was so far beyond his abilities it lay also beyond his understanding. (He had forgotten his experiences at Neu Brandenburg twenty-eight years before.) How was it possible that such a job had taken a household of young people the entire week? One of his students said, "We loved him because of his ideas but—sometimes—in spite of his personality."

The family tortoise was carried from Diemen in a cardboard box and let loose in the *Kortenhoeve* plot. It promptly disappeared. When an English poet arrived at the community, he found the Professor rummaging distractedly among the bushes.

"What are you looking for?"

"My turrdle! I have lost my turrdle!"

"Your—?"

"Turrdle! Turrdle!" He waved his hands in the air. "The word is English; why don't you know it?"

"Well, I'm sorry but I never—"

"It will fall into the water! We must be sure it does not drown!"

Light dawned. "Oh, a *turtle*. But they are water animals; they don't drown. Unless you mean a tortoise?" Colin pronounced the word the way it is spelt.

"I do not know that word! It is a turrdle, like I told you! It must not drown!"

While they searched, fruitlessly, Colin remembered that in America a tortoise is sometimes referred to as a turtle. That would explain the Professor's strange pronunciation; he must have learnt the word from an American.

When the first visit from Francis Schaeffer was due, Rookmaaker became increasingly unbearable, fussing round everyone's heels like a nervous hostess before the guests arrive. Everything had to be just so. One Worker got the rough edge of the Professor's tongue because the spotlights were not aimed correctly at the pictures on the living room wall. Another was reprimanded for not having finished laying the staircarpet. "The house had to be his own little showplace to impress Schaeffer," said one.

A student from Amsterdam remembered it from another angle: "I saw Rooky standing in the hallway. The place was in an uproar: floors being scrubbed, windows cleaned, piles of dishes being carried to and fro. Rooky stood there looking distinctly awkward, not quite knowing where he should put himself. Suddenly an idea flashed through his mind. Trying his hardest to look inconspicuous, he pulled a handkerchief from his pocket and then ever so sheepishly began to dust the top of the radiator."

The Reverend Schaeffer arrived, admired everything, preached, discussed and left. Rookmaaker swept the entire community away for a celebration meal in a Chinese restaurant where he ordered an elaborate dinner of many dishes. He beamed at the hungry students like an Oriental patriarch who has gathered his children around him. That evening he was exhausted. Others might have regained their composure in prayer, sleep or a gentle walk. Rookmaaker fled back to his studyful of books and letters the way a child runs back to the circle of comforting arms.

Rooky never forgot his former pupils, answering their letters deep into the night, his sloping handwriting leaving a wide left-hand margin, European-style, in which he added last-minute thoughts. Written Dutch (*schrijftaal*) is different from the spoken form, but when Rookmaaker wrote to a friend in English he simply chatted onto the page. To read the letters is to hear the light-textured, drawling voice.

His reply to one student in 1974 is full of fatherly concern for a man who was trying to integrate his music and his faith:

"As for your work. Indeed you need time. But unless you go popular it will be hard to find a place to do full time work. Yet it can come, if you produce things and people recognise your qualities. I feel the best way is just to be yourself. The rule is: you can never be better than you are. And don't try to be too *art*-conscious (in other words) self-conscious. Just make things with which you give something to others, like fine music. Not some snobbish fad-of-the-day.

"I'm sure the music you made in the past will never reach many—I'm not thinking about the big crowd, that has been mesmerised into the tinned commercial muzak of one kind or another—Kitsch!—but music that people will learn to love as the classics are loved. So just make good things— that you feel is right—don't compromise. Don't be afraid. If you succeed to break through—it's great. If not—yet some people may love it, and you yourself had the joy of making it. One never knows what's the outcome of what one is doing. And you can ask the Lord in this too."

Occasionally he would suggest something to prime the pump of a young artist whose ideas were in danger of running too much on theory:

"Just try to make what is in your head," he wrote to one. "You don't choose a style, you are a style. And give it a chance to develop. Maybe as a little diversion, try to compose some hymns, make a simple opera, e.g. Jesus at the well, or just a short story, make an overture. But just do."

He could discuss ideas in art till dawn rose over the Gelderland horizon but he did not allow his students to sit and theorise too long. "Well, your ideas may be good or they may be worthless. I cannot tell yet. And neither can you. Produce some work, a painting or a story or a poem. Put your ideas into something that is simple and real. Then we can talk about it and see if it worked."

Like every good teacher, Rooky knew his pupils, evaluating them at a distance the way he evaluated a picture, his brown eyes flicking over them. One student went to him with his problems and Rookmaaker was concerned and compassionate, the first time. Later, the man went again with the same complaints about life. This time his teacher turned on him in a rage, shaking and shouting, "If you don't buckle down you will go all through life giving up as soon as you have difficulties! You will get to sixty and do nothing with your life!"

His words were timely, as the student remembered: "He castigated me with such venom that he shook me to my senses. That was the last day that I was a dilettante."

If a student was in danger of experimenting too much, he emphasised the role of artistic tradition that every artist must build upon in each succeeding generation.

"You cannot begin as though there was nothing before you. There have been many who have struggled before you. Learn from them. Be humble. You stand on the shoulders of those others and you can maybe take their ideas a little further. That is all. Then one day someone will go beyond you. Only be sure that you take your ideas and your work deeper into the Christian way of seeing reality."

His concern was for the total life of his students and they responded by going to him with all problems of mind and heart. He wrote to a man about the girl who had been in his life:

"*If* you are meant for each other, I hope it works out well. Yet, it always means some work and action from the man's side particularly. Interest must be sustained, and shown. I can't give any advise here" (his English spelling was almost perfect) "but if you are passive it will go by, certainly. Courage and work—and may the Lord bless you."

A month later he was ready to bind up the wounds in that life:

"Thank you for your note. It is maybe sad but yet I feel it is wise not to go on with Luciana. She's so much younger, still immature. I really hope you'll find a good wife, somebody that can back you up, give you confidence. Pray for this; we do."

A young Christian friend was distressed by a marriage that had gone wrong. Before the engagement Rooky had taken him aside to say, "Veronica is not the right girl for you. You cannot have dual leadership in a marriage. The man must lead."

Now that events had proved him right, he did not stoop to say "I told you so", but bound up the broken reed. When they met, Rooky left the crowd, saying to Ted, "Come, let's go for a walk and maybe we have a drink in a café and talk. Now tell me how your life is going." He made himself his student's pastor in the best sense of that word. For many he was the only man they knew who, though he was not ordained, deserved the title.

An American college student dared to write about a jazz club that was being started by a small group of Christians. Would the Professor spare a moment to write and suggest what they could listen to, to start them off? Rookmaaker posted back a parcel of handwritten notes, xerox'd sheets from his files and notebooks, together with tapes of some of his own rare jazz records. No-one ever knew how many hours it had taken him to write, record and file the material. On the question of introducing jazz to the Christian world he was under no illusions. "I told you it would be difficult, didn't I?" he wrote to one friend.

His love of jazz formed a bridge with one man when other tastes were poles apart. In 1971 Pete Klausmeyer spent part of the winter in another European community but left before the three months were up, feeling that the time there was less than valuable. Two years later he applied to the community in the Netherlands hoping that the relative smallness of it would be a better experience.

He arrived at *Kortenhoeve* in summer 1974 and first caught sight of the Professor strolling across the gravel driveway outside the main house.

"It was late in the afternoon. The Rookmaakers had arrived sometime that day from Amsterdam and I remember he had on a medium grey suit and tie, which seemed out of the ordinary there since almost everyone wore jeans or something nearly as casual. He seemed quite relaxed and right at home, but nonchalant. I had the feeling right from the beginning that he was open and ready at any time to have a serious conversation with whomever happened along."

The two men soon found enormous differences of opinion. Rookmaaker loved the music of Heinrich Schütz and Bach, then almost nothing till early jazz. Pete's main interest was in music written after World War II. After living in the community for a while, he stopped asking questions and withdrew into himself. Rookmaaker noticed. During an evening discussion he looked across the room at the man from North Carolina and said severely, "You are too quiet!"

To Pete, the Professor seemed to have the view of a detached observer of music, an historian and a theorist. "I really couldn't see any value in someone devoting his whole life to *studying* art rather than *living* and *doing* it. I suppose I had hoped to find a sympathetic mind in Dr. Rookmaaker— one who would get down alongside of me and struggle *with* me. But what did I find? A stubborn Dutchman with archaic musical tastes and rock-hard opinions, who seemed to find much to dislike in twentieth-century culture!

"But I knew, even then, that there had to be some point of reconciliation since we were both Christians. However, that was the *only* common bond that I could see and not very clearly at that. But it was this very thought that kept me from dismissing Dr. R. as a hopeless reactionary who was entirely out of touch from where I stood. Here's a guy who loves the Lord, just as I'm trying to do. He can't be *all* bad!"

The summer ended and Pete returned home. A few letters began to pass between them and Rookmaaker's warmth and encouragement kept the small bond between them alive. The change in Pete came when he was away from *Kortenhoeve* and had time to do a lot of thinking. "I confess I didn't do much praying. But I just thought specifically about how and why two persons could be of the same faith and yet be so different. One thing that kept me from dismissing Dr. R. was that I knew he loved jazz."

But what kind of scholar was that: a man who loved early but not modern jazz, then skipped a couple of centuries back and picked out Schütz and Bach? As the Doctor of Music tried to come to terms with his time spent in *Kortenhoeve*, he re-read *Modern Art and the Death of a Culture.* "It was *so* hard for me to see that what I had devoted nearly eight years of my life to—graduate study in the craft of contemporary 'high-brow' composition—was being part of the twentieth-century death which Dr. R. comes to toward the end of his book. But I believe that what he says is true . . . and now my interest in electronic music has gone entirely."

The Professor's position forced him to rethink the importance of the elements of music, especially rhythm. Now he found himself striving for what was direct and clear, less in technique than in meaning. He composed a set of seven pieces for Baroque organ. "I strove for simplicity of expression, and I tried to make each piece a brief, tight statement. This is not too large a step, but it is a step, nevertheless. Perhaps in ten years from now, Lord willing, other things may show through."

Others had a similar experience in their own creative fields: initial dislike of Rookmaaker's teaching, then a slow mental shift, often with painful re-evaluation, and finally the fruit of Godly structures showing through their work. A painter recalled, "Rookmaaker said things about the Impressionists that annoyed me at the time, because it seemed they annoyed him. I was painting that way myself then and I felt he was saying everything I had done was worthless. In those days I saw a certain attractiveness in their technique. But now the Impressionists annoy me too. And now I see the fruits of something else beginning to come in my work." A film-maker was forced to reconsider camera technique after their talks. A goldsmith from Zürich took two years before her designs moved from surrealism to the deep realism of Rembrandt and Dürer.

From time to time Rookmaaker was wrenched away from his studies because of a friend's personal need. In September 1973, Dr. Kefa Sempangi with his wife fled from their home in Uganda for fear of being massacred by Idi Amin's soldiers. The couple was well known to Hans and Anky. Rookmaker had first met the Ugandan artist three years before when he saw a mural painting Kefa had done for the Lee Abbey Chapel in London. Kefa studied at the VU and when he had planned to return to Uganda in March, Anky was concerned.

"Your lives will not be safe there. Let us try to get you a safety ticket so you can get yourselves out." Without that ticket, their escape from Uganda would have been impossible. The refugees' re-entry into Holland in September 1973 was negotiated by Rookmaaker.

He worked long and tirelessly to get them political asylum in his country. He battled red tape to get the family a visa and arranged for their move to the U.S. to study. He went with Kefa to the U.S. Embassy in Den Haag with the proper accent and diplomatic skills to argue the case and he talked for an hour with a recalcitrant official in the passport office. In February 1974 Kefa took Penina and their child to safety in the States. Return to their own country would have been impossible. Kefa, who had been an art history teacher at Makerere University, had founded the Redeemed Church in Uganda. The church grew to a membership of fourteen thousand. His death would have been certain and brutal.

"Every February since then we have set aside a day to remember the Rookmaakers, of how God used them to have our lives spared from the brutal death of Amin's Nubian killers in Uganda.

"Many times I disagreed with Rookmaaker in art history seminars, but deep down we remained friends and he became supervisor for my doctrinal dissertation, 'Symbolism in African Art'. I couldn't understand how this man whose father had been a Governor in one of the Dutch colonies could be friendly with a foreign person like myself. Everything of my personal struggle became Rookmaaker's personal concern."

It was not the only time the Professor of *Kortenhoeve* had put himself out for a refugee. As JoAnn observed of that side of his nature, "He just killed himself for foreigners in trouble."

For all the kindred spirits he found through community work, Rookmaaker could fall into loneliness. Once he confided to Wim Rietkerk, "Graham is like a son to me but you have never become that way. I wonder why it is?"

"You do not see? Oh well, it is easy to see why. My own father, if he was still alive, would be about eighty years old. He was already middle-aged when I was born. So I think of you more as an older brother than a father." But he felt the explanation did not satisfy Rookmaaker.

When he had been immersed in the community work for two years, Hans Rookmaaker had sad family news: Hennie's husband had died of a heart attack. On the evening after the funeral Hans drove to *Kortenhoeve* to lead a seminar. He was still wearing his black suit and tie and he seemed subdued, as though touched by some emotion he was not able to file away. The seminar developed into a preaching session with Rookmaaker thumping repeatedly on the arm of his chair, "We've all got to take this seriously! These things are not a joke! The issues of life and death, they are real!"

In 1975 Hans and Anky moved to a house in Ommeren, a trim village near Eck-en-Wiel. Since they had first lived in Diemen, Amsterdam had grown to absorb the little suburb, but Ommeren was sunk deep in the countryside. Outside Hans' new study window the only sounds were the gaggle of a neighbour's ducks, the thump of an automatic bird-scarer and the creak of a bicycle being pedalled past the front garden.

That garden, front and back, expressed artistic rebellion

against the standards of neighbourhood plots. The Rookmaakers were inspired by a friend with organic gardening theories. They decided to let their land go completely wild for five years, then work with nature. After two years the tiny plot was a knee-high tangle of weeds and wild flowers. It was the delight of neighbourhood cats who danced a jig with grasshoppers and field-mice while the next door pony craned his neck over the fence to nibble the unsprayed grass.

Inside, the art Professor's home was pleasant and functional. Though the walls were hung with original paintings and a dozen house-plants graced the wide windowsill, the bookcases in the living room were grey metal and the lamps were the no-nonsense variety. Rookmaaker hated the romantic gleam of candlelight as much as he hated romance in any form.

One hot day in 1976 John, Graham and some others from the VU accepted Rookmaaker's invitation to review his seminars and suggest ways his teaching could be improved. They relaxed in the Ommeren living room and John teased the Professor about his weedy garden before they turned to business. There were criticisms of the level of scholarship in the material Rookmaaker was presenting at the VU. The students felt a fundamental weakness was that he never gave satisfactory criticism of the papers.

John told him, "I think it is because you are preoccupied with imparting a vision. You are not giving these people professional training. You are assuming a background and technical equipment that simply isn't there."

The rebuke was given lovingly and Rookmaaker knew it. In reply, he revealed a little of his heart: "I know I am very bad at criticising people. When I have done this in the past I have come over very heavy and crude. Good criticism is something I have never learnt how to do. It is my weakness. When I criticise I hurt people. Because I do not want to hurt, I do not say what I ought to say."

At the turn of 1976–77 there were tiny changes in him that his friends did not understand at the time. At Christmas 1976 an artist and his wife were driving near Ommeren.

170

"Shall we drop in and see Professor Rookmaaker?" "Oh, maybe not. I have no pressing questions just now. It would only be a social call and he is ill at ease with that kind of thing." But they turned the car towards Ommeren.

Anky welcomed them and bustled away to make coffee. Hans came down from his study and they sat on the brown leather chairs in the living room. It was the closest to a merely social chat they had ever known with him. Jan remembered, "He was quieter that day. He seemed interested in me more as a person, rather than as a man who paints pictures. He listened more."

In early January 1977 he was due to go to America again. Anky was unwell. "Oh, Hans, dear, I don't think you can go this time and leave me."

He was dumbfounded. "But how can I not go? It is my life."

"Yes, I see that. It is your whole life."

As he ended a prayer in the *Kortenhoeve* community that February, he said, "Lord Jesus, come soon." One of the students looked up with sudden clear-sight thinking, "This man's ready to meet Him. And I'm not."

In mid-February JoAnn visited *Kortenhoeve*. Rooky heard she was there and drove over from Ommeren just to see her. "He marched into the dining room where we were drinking tea and gave me a kiss on the cheek. I thought it was so strange, so warm; in a way, so unlike him. Almost as though he was saying goodbye."

The last person Rooky talked to at length was the American girl, Mattie. One Saturday in March 1977 they sat in his study in Ommeren from lunch to teatime, the book-lined room steadily filling with smoke. Mattie told him about the kind of Christianity she had met before.

"I guess I went along with them because I had nothing else and they seemed to offer me a different kind of magic."

"You were looking for magic?"

She made a wry face, "Maybe. Look—I'll tell you about me, but I'll understand if you say you want me to leave Eck-en-Wiel and you don't ever want to see me again."

"You have not told me anything yet."

"Well, I met these Christians and I guess they were kind of—charismatic? You know the kind? And they told me to just believe and I'd be saved and that was all I had to do."

"And did you?"

"Yes but"—she looked up miserably—"but it didn't work. And now I don't know if it is—was—true after all."

"Well, now you know there must also be the other side of the Gospel. There are responsibilities in living the Christian life. There are hard times, there are doubts." She was silent, so he told her briefly of his time in the Polish POW camp where his own Christian life had begun to move forward. This moment of confidence was rare. It was all she needed to begin to talk freely.

She dared to tell him how alcohol hadn't satisfied her, how sex had been destructive, how drugs were killing her so she could not bear to look at her own life. It was the story of many young lives in the sixties and seventies. Rooky had heard it many times before.

He listened like a rock, puffing his pipe slowly, his eyes on the Dürer print hanging on the right of his desk: *Combat of Virtue and Pleasure in the Presence of Hercules.* After a while he stirred in his chair. "Well, what you are telling me is a little thing after all."

"A little—!"

"I won't say it was right what you did, but it was such a small thing. When we stand before the Lord and have in our minds all those things that we thought were so terrible, they may be brushed aside. We may be asked, 'What about the time you didn't love this or this person? Or the time you didn't give the encouragement you could have given?' " He looked at her wisely, "I know you have been afraid."

"How do you know?"

"Pooh, that is not important. I know. But now you must not think of your outward actions but of the feelings of your heart when you were doing them. When these people said to you, 'Just believe' they were not right. But then when you look more deeply into the Gospel you will see that they were not wrong either." His Bible was open at John 3, a scent of

172

Schippers Tabac Speciaal rising from its pages. Verse 21 was underlined *'maar wie de waarheid doet, gaat tot het licht'* (he that does truth comes to the light). The word 'does' was encircled in pencil.

"I know these kind of people; they will tell you that you must have faith not works. But as you live with God you will find that the truth is not one or the other but both. Commitment is like crossing a bridge. Of course your heart is involved, but not your heart only. You ask your questions and you gather your information but at some point you have got to act on what you know. You cannot go on and on collecting information till you die or you'll never do anything with it.

"Your questions on doctrine have been important and we will go on trying to answer them. But at some point you have got to cross the bridge and on the other side is the road of the Christian life."

For a long moment he sat silent, toying with his pipe, his mind roaming back over his own road. It had begun in a solitary cell in Scheveningen, and he had followed it through Poland, the loss of Riekie, through a good, long marriage and over the rough and smooth of international prestige. The pampered Son of the Sumatra Resident had learnt a lot. He felt glad there would be more years ahead and still more to learn.

Mattie watched his face lift into a smile that filled the whole room. "I cannot tell you how good or how exciting or how wonderful that road is till you cross the bridge. But when you cross it you will begin to find out."

"Someone so Human"

ON MARCH 5th 1977 Hans let himself through his front door and started up the stairs to his study. Once he had done this after a three-week lecture tour in America. This time, Anky came through the hall from the living room and caught him. She did not want to sound like his mother but there are times when you must ask a direct personal question.

"Well? What did the specialist say?"

"Good news. He cannot find anything wrong with me."

"I didn't think there was anything wrong with you. You are as healthy as a horse. You only need a little more rest."

"He said that too, but it's impossible. Still, he checked my heart, blood pressure, everything, and said I am fit. I wasn't worried but it is nice to know. I told him I was willing to do anything except cut down on food or tobacco."

"And he told you to cut down on food and tobacco?"

He shuffled his big feet. "Maybe I could eat a little less well."

The specialist was a personal friend who had agreed to do the check-up when Anky reminded her husband that he was about to have another birthday, his fifty-fifth. On that birthday, he had suddenly confided to Winnie, "I feel restless. I have been studying the same subject for thirty years. I need a new career, something different to learn. What do you suggest?"

Winnie had teased him. "You ought to go on to an American TV talk-show, Professor."

But he would not be laughed out of his sombre mood, repeating, "I need a new career." He had three weeks to live.

February 27th fell close to Kees' twenty-first birthday so

they all agreed to combine the celebration with a family meal. Hans the son came with his wife and little Hinko, making three generations of Rookmaakers at the Jugo-slavische Restaurant Vladimir on the Amsteldijk. They chose from a menu featuring Beroemde Sumedinka and exotic dishes of lamb and yogurt.

Dora leaned across the table, her brown eyes beaming affectionately. "You are looking well, Hansje, but you are looking too fat!"

"Ah, Doortje, tomorrow I will begin to cut down. Tonight we celebrate. Now call the waiter, Aagje, and let us find out what some of these strange things are made of. Or shall we order something we have never heard of? What do you think? Doortje, I hardly ever see you these days. Come and visit me in Ommeren."

"No. I don't have time."

"Remember when we were children you always told me, 'You are not allowed to say no'?"

"Hah! I'm your sister. I can say it to you!" If brother and sister had known it was to be their last evening on earth together they would not have enjoyed it.

Now the specialist had given him a clean bill of health and he put the matter of age out of his mind. There were letters on his desk, plans for a lecture on the nature of reality and notes for the forthcoming book on God's hand in history. He was putting together a tape recording for Graham: examples of New Orleans clarinettists and some pieces by George Lewis, the Armstrong Hot Seven and Jelly-Roll Morton. He wrote to his beloved Birmingham painters asking for slides of their recent work and suggesting another exhibition at the VU. It was a busy week.

That Sunday, March 13th, Hans and Anky drove to the *Kortenhoeve* chapel where Wim preached on I Corinthians 1:18: "the preaching of the cross is to them that perish foolishness; but to us who are saved it is the power of God."

"Once upon a time," Wim told the congregation, "there was a village fair that was due to open in the evening. Everything was ready and the villagers were at home getting ready for the great event. A fire started to burn in the fairground tents and it spread dangerously near to the village itself. The clown in his ridiculous hair and funny shoes rushed from house to house, warning the people, pleading with tears to get away before it was too late. 'That is a good joke!' they said, That is an original joke!' The more he urged them to believe him, the more they laughed till the fire spread further and destroyed them all."

Wim spoke each paragraph first in Dutch, then repeated it in English for the benefit of foreigners at *Kortenhoeve*. "The preaching of the Gospel sounds like the foolishness of that clown," he told them, "People listen, but do they take it seriously enough to let themselves be changed? We seem to them like a clown crying for the danger, but the danger is real."

"For once," Wim remembered afterwards, "Professor Rookmaaker listened to the sermon." Didn't he always? "Well, honestly no. There were times when he looked as if to say, 'Yes, yes, I have heard most of this before. I will listen better with my eyes closed.' He would nod off. But that Sunday he sat with his eyes on me the whole time and his mouth a little open as if he was learning something interesting and new."

After the service there was something on his mind. "Wim, I have a letter from someone who asks for advice. He is a Jim from Canada. I have searched in my mind but I cannot remember a Jim from Canada."

Wim thought hard about the stream of blue-jeaned people who had begun to walk the Christian road at *Kortenhoeve*. "Could it be that English Jim who emigrated there? No, I wonder if it was the very tall Jim, you remember him? The one who helped to build the chicken house."

The Professor shook his head. The March breeze outside the chapel stirred a strand of his thin silver hair and the line of poplar trees shook their branches like pinions. "It was not that Jim, I am sure. Help me remember, Wim. I want to answer the letter but I cannot do it properly if I cannot remember his background. Maybe tomorrow the answer will come."

That afternoon, back in the house in Ommeren, he did not

feel well. There was a tightness in his chest that moved towards his jaw. Rooky knocked out his pipe and laid it on the living room table, then he put his feet up on the brown sofa. Above him on the wall hung his choice of picture for the family living room: an original from the school of de Witte, showing a group of figures standing in the take-it-or-leave-it ice coldness of a seventeenth-century Reformed church interior.

He dozed and woke to watch the Sunday news on television. On top of the television set was a bronze figure of a guinea pig by Joe McTaggart, one of his Edinburgh friends. Anky had once declared she would rather have that loving little sculpture than all the paintings in the room. Outside the house the landscape was fresh and bright, the details clear into the distance as in the work of de Koninck and Hobbema. The Professor thought about the letters on his desk upstairs. If only he could remember who that Jim was; a person's background made such a difference in the way their questions must be answered. He needed more time to put his ideas into writing. He had a drawerful of unfinished manuscripts.

At five to eight that evening he put his hand to his chest saying, "Now I really am not at all well." It was a simple death.

His face was caught in an expression of surprise and delight and complete absorption as though he was saying, "So. I am dead. Well, that is an interesting thing to happen. Now let me see what I can learn."

His funeral was that Wednesday in the pre-Reformation church in Eck-en-Wiel. Partway through the service the walls quivered to the rock beat of a Mahalia Jackson recording, "I'm gonna move on up a little higher". Anky had made a point of having it included.

Wim preached on Revelation 14:13: "Blessed are the dead which die in the Lord . . . and their works do follow them." Afterwards four hundred young people followed the coffin to the grave. Elderly men from Eck-en-Wiel village lifted the coffin from the car. They stood for a moment on the rising ground, their top-hats and tailcoats silhouetted against the sky. It was like a scene from an Ingmar Bergman film. Then Hans Roelof Rookmaaker was lowered into the sandy soil of Gelderland, where the Rijn delta has drained the northwest corner of Europe since unrecorded time. The figure had returned to his landscape.

The news broke like a clap of thunder on a fair day. One British art student sobbed when he heard his teacher had gone. A Dutch pastor, looking even more sober than usual, said, "But there are still one or two things I wanted to ask him." Dora sighed, "He is going too soon."

In London the following Saturday, one of Rooky's Inter-Varsity friends summed up his ministry in a few words: "It is wonderful how God can use someone so human."

APPENDIX I

Source Material

Biography
Johanna-Ruth Dobschiner, *Selected to Live*; Pickering and Inglis 1969
Anne Frank, *The Diary of Anne Frank*; transl. B. M. Mooyaart. Doubleday, Pan Books 1945

Geography
George C. Carter, *Man and the Land* 2nd ed.; Holt, Rinehart and Winston 1968
Jean Gottmann, *A Geography of Europe*; Henry Holt U.S. 1951
Audrey M. Lambert, *The Making of the Dutch Landscape*; Seminar Press N.Y. 1971

History
A. J. Baker, *Behind Barbed Wire*; B. T. Batsford 1974
G. Kitson Clark, *The Critical Historian*; Heinemann 1967
R. C. K. Ensor, *A Miniature History of the War*; O.U.P. 1944
Williston Walker, *A History of the Christian Church*; Scribners N.Y. 1959
The War Illustrated: Amalgamated Press n.d.

History of Art
E. H. Gombrich, *The Story of Art*; Phaidon 11th edn. 1966
Hans R. Rookmaaker, *Art and the Public Today*; L'Abri Fellowship Foundation 1969
Hans R. Rookmaaker, *Modern Art and the Death of a Culture*; IVP 1970

Indonesia
Keith Buchanan, *The Southeast Asian World*; G. Bell and Sons Ltd. 1967
Foder, *Guide to Japan and East Asia*; Hodder and Stoughton 1970
Maslyn Williams, *Five Journeys from Jarkarta*; Collins 1966

179

Jazz, Blues and Dance

Gilbert Chase, *America's Music* rev. 2nd edn. McGraw-Hill N.Y. 1955

LeRoi Jones, *Blues People, Negro Music in White America*; MacGibbon and Kee 1963

Orrin Keepnews and Bill Grover Jr., *A Pictorial History of Jazz*; Spring Books 1968

Frances Rust, *Dance in Society*; Routledge and Kegan Paul 1969

Nazi Germany

William Sheridan Allen, *The Nazi Seizure of Power*; Eyre and Spottiswoode 1966

Robert Cecil, *The Myth of the Master Race*; B. T. Batsford 1972

Richard Hanser, *Prelude to Terror, the Rise of Hitler 1919–1923*; Rupert Hart-Davis 1971

Joseph C. Harsch, *Pattern of Conquest*; Heinemann 1942

Richard Grunberger, *Germany 1918–1945*; B. T. Batsford 1964

Richard Grunberger, *A Social History of the Third Reich*; Weidenfeld and Nicolson 1971

Netherlands

A. J. Barnouw, *The Making of Modern Holland*; Allen and Unwin 1948

Vincent Brome, *Europe's Free Press*; Feature Books Ltd 1934

J. J. Boolen and Dr. J. C. van der Does, *Five Years of Occupation*; The Secret Press of D.A.V.I.D. 1945

Foder, *Guide to Holland*; Hodder and Stoughton 1975

Pieter Geyl, *History of the Low Countries*; Macmillan 1964

Ann Hoffmann, *The Dutch: How they live and work*; David and Charles 1971

Alan C. Jenkins, *The Golden Band, Holland's Fight against the Sea*; Methuen 1966

Sigfried J. Laet, *The Low Countries* (ed. Glyn Daniel); Thames and Hudson 1958

Lucas van der Land ed., *Delta, A Review of the Arts, Life and Thought in the Netherlands*; Delta, Amsterdam 1967

Walter B. Maass, *The Netherlands at War 1940–1945*; Abelard-Schuman 1970

Max Schuchart, *The Netherlands*; Thames and Hudson 1972

William Z. Shetter, *The Pillars of Society, Six Centuries of Civilisation in the Netherlands*; Martinus Nijhoff, The Hague 1971

Other Sources

Catholic Central Library, Imperial War Museum and Netherlands Embassy, London; Jewish Historical Museum, Amsterdam.

Unpublished taped lectures by HRR between 1971 and 1977.

My thanks to Dhr. Menger for his help with Chapters Six and Eight, to Kees Rookmaaker for information on the Komodo Dragon and Mertens frog, to Hans van Seventer for finding the poem "Zorghvliet" for Chapter Five, to Tony Wales and to my husband for correcting the final MS and to the following people who shared letters, memories, and information:

Oliver Barclay
Dr. Graham M. Birtwistle
Patricia Bletcher
Dhr. Brouwer
Dr. Edward Clowney
Paul and Tessa Clowney
Minna Cornelisse
Les Cunliffe
Tim Dean
Henneke De Miranda
Meryl Doney
Margaret Dougan
Colin and Barbara Duriez
William Edgar
Nigel Goodwin
Dr. David R. Hanson
Anton Jaanse
Marc de Klijn
Peter Klausmeyer
Jan van Loon
Sean McCormick
Simon Morgan

Wendy Morrison
Judy Peterson
Coxie Priester
Drs. Wim Rietkerk and
    Greta Rietkerk
Revd. Francis A. Schaeffer
Dr. Kefa Sempangi
Hans and JoAnn van Seventer
Peter S. Smith
James W. Sire
Tony Wales
John and Maria Walford
Denis Weber
Bob and Geertsma Wielenga
Carl Woodson

Special thanks to members of the family who shared their personal memories and gave their support to this project: Anky Rookmaaker-Huitker, Hans Rookmaaker, L. C. Rookmaaker, Marleen Hengelaar, Dora Haver Droese and Hennie Rotgans.

"(Historical imagination) can reveal much that the process of research, however ingeniously its results may be manipulated by mathematics, can never reveal. This is particularly true of the personal experiences of human beings and the things which have moved their minds and spirits. Men's actions can be the subject of detailed research and enumerated, so, with much less certainty, can the influences which possibly affected their actions and so can their words. But what went on in their minds escapes exact scrutiny and classification. It can only be known by inference, and to understand it, if it is to be understood at all, intuition and imagination are necessary; it can never be discovered by means of the mere accumulation of detail, however massive that accumulation may be."

G. Kitson Clark, *The Critical Historian*

Publications by H. R. Rookmaaker

1959 *Synthetist art theories.* Genesis and nature of the ideas on art of Gauguin and his circle. Academisch Proefschrift . . . university of Amsterdam. Amsterdam.

1960 *Jazz, blues, spirituals.* Wageningen. (In Dutch.)

1962 *Kunst en amusement.* Kampen.

1965 *De kunstenaar een profeet?* (Text of inaugural lecture.) Kampen.

1968 *Art and the public today.* Huemoz (second edition 1969)— includes *De kunstenaar een profeet?*

1970 *Modern art and the death of a culture.* London, reprinted 1970, 1973; Japanese 1974, French 1974.

1972 *Gauguin and 19th century art theory.* Amsterdam (new edition of (1959) with new preface and a few additions to the bibliography).

1974 *Is het nodig modern te zijn om bij de tijd te zijn?* pp. 69–111 *in*: Macht en onmacht van de twintigste eeuw. Amsterdam.

1977 *Art needs no justification.* London (Dutch translation 1978).

Index

73

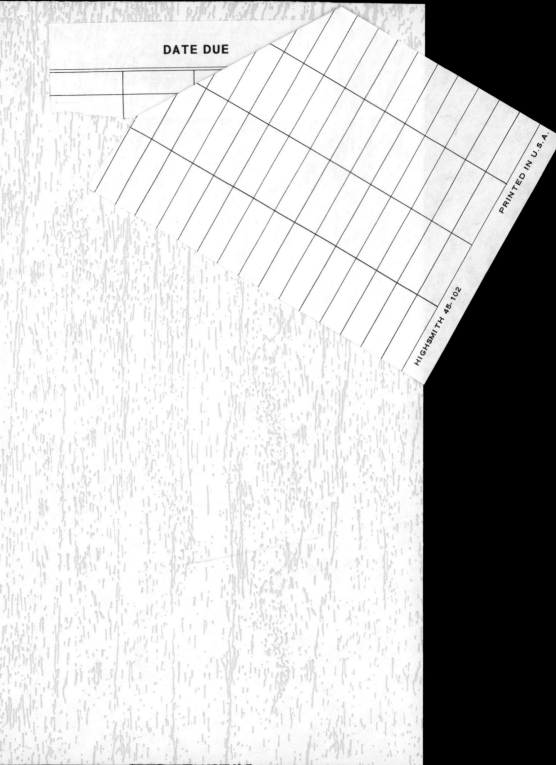

DATE DUE